ALSO BY HELEN VENDLER

INHABIT THE POEM

Inhabit the Poem
Last Essays

Helen Vendler

LIBRARY OF AMERICA

Inhabit the Poem: Last Essays
by Helen Vendler
is published with support from

JOHN STAUFFER
and
THE HARVARD
UNIVERSITY ENGLISH
DEPARTMENT

For Leon Wieseltier, dear friend

Contents

Preface

IN TEACHING, I was happiest when I saw students (rarely exposed to any poetry) understanding two indispensable constituents of a lyric poem: its originality and its uncanny embodiment of feelings. For earlier civilizations, "poetry" had often meant "long narrative poetry"—now renamed, in its early forms, "epic poetry"—which included the actions of both human beings and gods. But as culture became more secular, narrative increasingly took on the form of prose, and "poetry" gradually came to mean short poems about human feelings. By 1800, in the second edition of his *Lyrical Ballads,* Wordsworth could claim that "poetry is passion: it is the history or science of feelings." The simple definition comes first: "*Poetry is passion.*" But Wordsworth immediately, in the very same sentence, subdivides his definition: "*it is the history* or *science of feelings.*" Is "or science" an afterthought or an equal partner? Does poetry generate two basic genres, one that exposes a first-person history of feelings—"My heart aches"—while the other (often voiced in the impersonal "one" or "we") attempts an analysis of "universal" human emotions: "Here, where men sit and hear each other groan." My two quotations occur within the same poem, Keats's "Ode to a Nightingale," suggesting that a personal narrative of feelings is often assisted by one or another analytic means. At any moment, passion may be narrating itself or analyzing itself, and although it is tempting to reduce a poem to its human first-person pathos, that reduction falsifies it.

The poet Allen Tate once said of Keats's "To Autumn"

that it "is a very nearly perfect piece of style but it has lit-
tle to say." I thought it had everything to say about human
life and death and much in between, and wrote a book
on Keats's odes to show how style—at every level from
punctuation to grammar to sentence-mode to rhetoric
to stanza-shape to illustration and allusion to rhyme and
rhythm—is always "saying," with the incomparable pre-
cision of poets. Poetry, for Wordsworth, is, then, passion
embodied by narrative or analysis. It must track the his-
tory of feelings and explain how the language chosen by
the poet incarnates an analysis of the origin and evolution
of such feelings.

Poems are often taught as statements expressible in
a summary form: "My love for you will never change"
(Shakespeare, Sonnet 116) or "Christianity is dead; we find
instead a form of secular and changing faith in the natu-
ral world" (Wallace Stevens, "Sunday Morning"). They
are rarely presented as works of art—as a ballet would
be described by a report on its choreography, its number
of dancers, and its relation to earlier genres of ballet and
ballet-music. But that is how temporal artworks are com-
posed, whether dance, or music, or poetry: they are forms
evolving as they go, usually changing their mind as they
go along, often ending somewhere quite far (intellectu-
ally speaking) from where they began. The intrinsic drama
of lyric poetry is constituted by the constant volatility of
consciousness as well as by its occasional stabilization.

THE DRAMA of reading poetry arises in the moment when
all its components "click" into shape, relating all to each,
as a sudden shaft of light illuminates the poem as a whole.
There are readings which are "wrong"—through igno-
rance, as when a German critic interpreted Shakespeare's

praise of love ("It is the star to every wand'ring bark") in terms of "the pathetic animal cry" in lieu of Shakespeare's intended "barque," meaning "ship," a symbol borrowed from Petrarch's love poetry—or when a student confuses "cast out" with a fishing "cast." In short, every reader begins in ignorance, but continued reading brings the increase in cultural and linguistic awareness necessary to finer perceptions and better speculations.

Today's readers, while often feeling powerfully attracted by a poem, need to have someone—a friend, an author, a teacher—to supply an awareness they may not yet possess—of an etymology, or the implications of a change from third-person to first-person expression, or the plot of a myth. Students' faces light up once they see a way into a poem in the wake of their expanded reach:

> These things, these things were here and but the
>   beholder
> Wanting; which two when they once meet,
> The heart rears wings bold and bolder
> And hurls for him, O half hurls earth for him off
>   under his feet.

At fifteen, I discovered that instant conjunction of mind and marvelous object, and wanted to find out what made it happen. Like Hopkins, I found that each successful artwork is unique, and with Yeats I was sure that only idiosyncratic style confers uniqueness. One recognizes a style and says, "That's Milton" or "That's Mahler." Only some poems radiate idiosyncratic style; the rest are made by what Pope scorned as "the mob of gentlemen that wrote with ease," whose works fade into anonymity. The popular belief that "gatekeepers"—publishers, university lecturers, anthologists, and advertisers—create the longevity of the authors we call "canonical" is false. The writers who last well beyond their own era persist because other serious writers have admired them: Chaucer admired Boccaccio, Spenser admired Chaucer, Milton admired Spenser, Wordsworth admired Milton, Keats admired Wordsworth, Yeats admired Keats, and so on down to our own day.

What great authors admire in each other is above all their eager and difficult renovation of language through style. Even great talent can be frustrated, as we know, by absence of education, discouragement by publishers, poverty, and social discrimination. Talent withers, or is disregarded, or disappoints expectation. There is always more mediocrity than radiance in the verse of every era. But against such difficulties, there arise, to our joy, a Whitman (who became a poet by being first a printer) and a Dickinson (whose father owned more books than the library of Amherst College). We have only to wait, and "the canon," sifted by centuries, slowly establishes itself.

WHEN LEON WIESELTIER founded *Liberties: A Journal of Culture and Politics*, and asked me to be a regular contributor, I told him that I would like to write for each issue a comment on a single poem. He enthusiastically agreed. I decided to write only on poets no longer living (so as not to make invidious choices) and to call up additional poems only rarely. In all but two instances I kept to those principles: I wrote on a living poet (Ocean Vuong) and I tracked in several poems beginning with Emily Brontë's "No coward soul is mine" an innovation in lyrical abstraction.

My poetic examples here range historically from Donne

to Vuong; geographically from England to the United States to Ireland; and generically from common forms (elegy, sonnet, prophecy) to more unexpected ones (the representation of a mad mind, an inventory of commercial receipts). In many of the commentaries there is a forensic purpose: I want to refute misreadings of some famous poems (by Donne, by Yeats, by Whitman) or introduce an entirely new reading (of Blake's "The Lamb," for instance). But my principal hope was to bring to other readers the intense pleasure of grasping the full resonance of a significant poem. For each of these poems, I hope to cast light on its imaginative originality; its escapes from cliché, intellectual mediocrity, and linguistic inertia; and its ambitious adventures in linguistic play as it searches out, for its own era, the passionate and permanent feelings of the human race.

Loosed Quotes

The Second Coming

Turning and turning in the widening gyre
The falcon cannot hear the falconer;
Things fall apart; the centre cannot hold;
Mere anarchy is loosed upon the world,
The blood-dimmed tide is loosed, and everywhere
The ceremony of innocence is drowned;
The best lack all conviction, while the worst
Are full of passionate intensity.

Surely some revelation is at hand;
Surely the Second Coming is at hand.
The Second Coming! Hardly are those words out
When a vast image out of *Spiritus Mundi*
Troubles my sight: somewhere in sands of the desert
A shape with lion body and the head of a man,
A gaze blank and pitiless as the sun,
Is moving its slow thighs, while all about it
Reel shadows of the indignant desert birds.
The darkness drops again; but now I know
That twenty centuries of stony sleep
Were vexed to nightmare by a rocking cradle,
And what rough beast, its hour come round at last,
Slouches towards Bethlehem to be born?

W. B. YEATS

Turning and turning in the widening gyre
The falcon cannot hear the falconer;
Things fall apart; the centre cannot hold;
. . . . .
The best lack all conviction, while the worst
Are full of passionate intensity.

I N EVERY CRISIS they appear, those famous and familiar lines from "The Second Coming," written in 1919 by W. B. Yeats. Journalists and critics alike seem to take them as final assertions of Yeats's own beliefs. Such innocent judgments do not ask why those lines open the poem, or for how long their assertions remain asserted. The poem itself has become lost behind the quotability of its opening lines. And Yeats, it seems, wants to be a pundit.

In our ready "yes, yes" to those lines, we think we are accepting the judgment of a sage, but by the time we reach the close of the poem—which is a question, not an assertion—we are driven to imagine the changing states of the writer composing this peculiar poem, and we raise questions. What feelings required Yeats to change his bold initial stance, and in what order did those feelings arise? In order to understand this poem, to free it from its ubiquitous misuses, and to restore it to both its opening grandeur and its subsequent humiliation, those are the questions that we must answer.

Yeats was an inveterate reviser of his own ever-laborious writing: recalling his difficulty in composing "The Circus Animals' Desertion," he confesses, "I sought a theme and sought for it in vain, / I sought it daily for six weeks or so." (Mention of that poem in his letters of the time proves this no exaggeration: I counted the weeks.) What was the obstacle suspending his progress? (He spends the poem finding out.) In "Adam's Curse" he remarks in frustration, "A line will take us hours maybe . . ." Hours to do what? ". . . to articulate sweet sounds together." Yeats puts the sequence of sounds first; he composed by ear. Are the resulting sounds always "sweet" in the ordinary sense of the word? Not at all; but they are "sweet" in the internal order of rhythms and styles as the poem evolves. When the poet has articulated its theme, its sounds, and its lines to the best of his powers, the ear registers its satisfaction.

"The Second Coming" is a lurid refutation of the lurid Christian expectations of the Second Coming of Christ, which Jesus himself foretells in Matthew 24:29–30:

> Immediately after the tribulation of those days shall the sun be darkened, and the moon shall not give her light, and the stars fall from heaven, and the powers of the heavens shall be shaken:

> And then shall appear the sign of the Son of man in heaven: and then shall all the tribes of the earth mourn, and they shall see the Son of man coming in the clouds of heaven with great power and great glory.

Yeats proposes a surreal alternative to Jesus's prophecy, proposing that on the Last Day we will see not Christ in majesty but a menacing, pitiless, and coarse beast who "slouches towards Bethlehem to be born." "After us the Savage God," Yeats had said as early as 1896. He watched through the decades, appalled by the sequential horror of world events: the World War from 1914 to 1918, the failed Easter Rising in Ireland in 1916, the Bolshevik Revolution in 1917. And his first assertions in "The Second Coming" are indeed thoughts prompted by such political upheavals (and by earlier ones—Marie Antoinette appears in the drafts).

But what sort of assertions does he choose to express his thoughts? After the octave of assertions, there is a break not entirely accounted for, since the whole poem is not written in regular stanzas, and there are no further breaks. The compressed sentiments preceding the break are undermined by the unexplained and increasing mystery of the poet's phrases, bringing the reader into the perplexity of the poet. The whole octave is full of riddles: What is a *gyre*? *Whose* is the falcon? What is the *centre* the center of? Why all the passive verbs? Who loosed the anarchy? Whose *blood*, *loosed* by whom, has dimmed what tide? What is meant by *the ceremony of innocence*? Who are *the best* and who are *the worst*? Such abstract language, such invisible agents, and such unascribed actions persist in Yeats's opening declarations, down to the period that closes the octave.

The quotability of Yeats's opening passage derives, of course, from the total and unmodified confidence of its initial reportage, impersonal and unrelenting, offering a naked list of present-tense events happening "everywhere." Stripped to their kernels, these are Yeats's truculently unmitigated hammer-blows of grammar:

The falcon cannot hear
Things fall apart
The centre cannot hold
Mere anarchy is loosed
The blood-dimmed tide is loosed
Everywhere the ceremony of innocence is drowned

The best lack all conviction
The worst are full of passionate intensity

The break, after Yeats's introductory eight-line block, leads an educated reader to expect that a six-line block will follow, completing a sonnet. Yet the poet finds himself unable to maintain his original jeremiad, which has been aggressive, omniscient, panoramic, and prophetic. Yeats "begins over again," and utters in the fourteen lines following the break a complete second "sonnet," a *rifacimento* of the one originally intended, in which he rejects his earlier rhetoric of impersonal omniscience as inauthentic from his human lips. Who is he to speak as though he could see the world with the panoramic scan proper only to God? That so many successive writers have been eager to reissue his lines reveals how greatly the human mind is seduced by the vanity of the unequivocal. Can we requote without unease what the poet himself immediately rejected?

Although "The Second Coming" begins with an attempt at couplet-rhyme, soon—as Peter Sacks has pointed out to me—the couplets begin to disintegrate, as though they themselves were intent on demonstrating how "things fall apart." After the break, Yeats reveals in its wake a second attempt at a fourteen-line sonnet, one exhibiting a traditional "spillover" octave of nine lines (implying overmastering emotion in the writer) before a truthful closing "sestet" of five lines, making up the desired fourteen. The second, revisionary octave replaces the certainty of the poet's original octave with the self-defensive uncertainty of "Surely." Longing for a revelation more humanly reliable than an unsupported façade of godlike prophecy, Yeats insistently utters his second "Surely," one no less dubious than the first. The second "Surely" attempts to locate a cultural myth to which he can attach the vision vouchsafed to him in a revelation arising within his human consciousness. "Surely the Second Coming is at hand. / The Second Coming!"

For the first time in the poem, we hear Yeats speaking in the first person, declaring that "a vast image out of *Spiritus Mundi* / Troubles my sight." The poet is the sole spectator of this vast image, and he claims that it stems not from his own bodily sense of sight but from the World Spirit, a universal *Spiritus Mundi* always potentially able to rise into human awareness. (Poets so often describe the initial inspiration for a poem as something coming unbidden that the reader is not troubled by Yeats's myth of a World Spirit supplying the image for his revelation.) The poet has decided that it is more honest, more tenable, to write in the first person, to present himself as one whose imagination has reliably generated a telling and trustworthy "vast image" of his historical moment. He has forsaken his impressive but fraudulent rhetoric of omniscience for an account of his private inspiration.

Once Yeats has repudiated his initial "divine" posture as a guaranteed seer-of-everything-everywhere, he can take on, in the first person, his limited historical image-making self and create with it a "human" sestet for his newly "remade" sonnet. Admitting the fallibility of any transient metaphorical image, he acknowledges that his image vanishes, "The darkness drops again," and he is left alone. Yet he grandly maintains, in spite of his abandoning a prophetic stance, that he now definitely "knows" something.

The "something" turns out to be a single historical fact:

the exhaustion of Christian cultural authority after its "twenty centuries" of rule. His "vast image"—its nature as yet unspecified—has shown him that Christianity will be replaced by a counterforce, a pagan one. Drawing on his reading of Vico and Herbert Spencer, Yeats believed that history exhibited repetitive cycles of opposing forces. Just as Christianity overcame the preceding centuries of Egypt and Greece, now it is time for some power to defeat Christianity.

In his private "revelation" the poet has seen the Egyptian stone sphinx asleep "somewhere" in sands of a desert. (The uncertain "somewhere" admits the loss of the initial "everywhere" of Yeats's prophetic opening.) The "stony sleep" of the Sphinx has lasted through the twenty centuries of Christianity, but now Fate has set an anticipatory cradle rocking in Bethlehem, birthplace of the previous god, and a sphinx-like creature rouses itself to claim supremacy:

> The darkness drops again; but now I know
> That twenty centuries of stony sleep
> Were vexed to nightmare by a rocking cradle . . .

Although the poet "knows" that Christianity is undergoing the nightmare of its death-throes, he cannot declare with any confidence what will replace it. He can no longer boast "I know that . . .": he can merely ask a speculative question which embodies his own mixed reaction of fear and desire to the vanishing of a now outworn Christianity, the only ideological system he has ever known. What will replace the Jesus of Bethlehem, he asks, and invents a brutal and unaesthetic divinity, a sphinx seen in glimpses —"with lion body and the head of a man, / A gaze blank and pitiless as the sun." The "desert birds" (formerly, it is implied, perched at rest on the immobile stone of the Egyptian statue) are now disturbed by the unexpected arousal of the "slow thighs" beneath them. The indignant birds, their movement in the sky inferred from their agitated cast shadows, "reel about," disoriented, projecting, as surrogates, the poet's own indignation as he guesses at the future parallel upheaval of his own world. Unable to be prophetic, unable now even to say "Surely," the poet ends his humanly authentic but still unsatisfied sestet with a speculative question, one that fuses by alliteration "beast" and "Bethlehem" and "born":

And what rough beast, its hour come round at last,
Slouches towards Bethlehem to be born?

A CONVENTIONAL reading of the poem might take us this far. But no one, so far as I know, has commented that the culminating and ringing phrase, "its hour come round at last," is an allusion to Jesus's famous statement to his mother at the wedding feast at Cana. When she points out to her son that their host has run out of wine, he rebukes her as he had once done in his youth when she had lost him in Jerusalem and found him preaching to the rabbis in the temple: "Wist ye not that I must be about my Father's business?" (Luke 2:49). At Cana, Jesus is even harsher as he tells his mother that he is not yet willing to manifest his divinity: "Woman, what have I to do with thee? mine hour is not yet come." Not answering her son's austere question, she simply says to the servants, "Whatsoever he saith unto you, do it." He tells them to fill their jugs with water, yet when they pour it is wine that issues, as, in silent obedience to his mother, Jesus performs his first miracle, even though to do so means changing his own design of when he will reveal his divinity. The evangelist comments: "This beginning of miracles did Jesus in Cana of Galilee, and manifested forth his glory" (John 2:4–5, 11). Unlike Jesus, who wished to delay his hour of divine manifestation, Yeats's "rough beast" has been impatiently awaiting his own appointed hour, and it has come. His allusion to Jesus's "mine hour is not yet come" establishes a devastating parallel between the rough beast's presumed divinity and that of Jesus, as the poet quails before the savage god of the future.

One senses there must be a literary bridge between the glorious "hour" of Jesus and the hideous hour of the rough beast. As so often, one finds the link in Shakespeare. In *Henry V*, Shakespeare alludes to Jesus's remark, but adds the malice and impatience that will be incorporated by Yeats in his image of the rough beast. A French noble at Agincourt describes, in prospect, the vulturous hovering of crows waiting to attack the corpses of the English who will have died in battle. Eager for their expected feast on English carrion, "their executors, the knavish crows, / Fly o'er them all, impatient for their hour." We know that the rough beast has been, like the crows, "all impatient for [his] hour," because, once loosed on the world, he knows that his appointed hour, long craved by him, has come "at last." Yeats had been alluding to Jesus's words about the appointed hour ever since 1896: in his youthful poem "The Secret Rose," a benign apocalypse is ushered in by the idealized romance symbol of the rose. He even remembered—writing in 1919—his original inscription of the longing word "Surely" in the envisaged victory of the Secret Rose:

> Surely thine hour has come, thy great wind blows,
> Far-off, most secret, and inviolate Rose?

"Surely thine hour has come," "Surely some revelation is at hand": apocalyptic symbols thread their way through Yeats's life-work. In the same volume as "The Secret Rose," we find a contrastively violent version of the End Times, drawing on the sinister Irish legend of a battle in "The Valley of the Black Pig" ushering in what Yeats called "an Armageddon which shall quench all things in the Ancestral Darkness again." Just as the brave warrior Cuchulain—in Yeats's deathbed poem, "Cuchulain Comforted"—must be reincarnated as a coward to complete his knowledge of life, so the serene beauty of the Secret Rose must, to be complete, coexist with a twin, a wildness of apprehension. Maud Gonne, whom Yeats loved in frustration all his life, incarnated for him the conjunction of wildness and beauty:

> But even at the starting post, all sleek and new,
> I saw the wildness in her and I thought
> A vision of terror that it must live through
> Had shattered her soul.

Maud had already appeared in 1904 as the paradoxical "Quiet . . . eating her wild heart" (an image of wild love borrowed from the opening sonnet of Dante's *La Vita Nuova*). She is the female companion to another apocalyptic creature, the Sagittarius of the zodiac; he is a Great Archer poised, his bow drawn, in the woods of Lady Gregory's estate. He, like Shakespeare's predatory birds, "but awaits His hour" to loose arrows upon a degenerate Ireland, where English archaeologists are sacrilegiously excavating sacred Tara and the ignorant Dublin masses are actually celebrating the coronation in England of Edward VII:

> I am contented, for I know that Quiet
> Wanders laughing and eating her wild heart
> Among pigeons and bees, while that Great Archer,
> Who but awaits His hour to shoot, still hangs
> A cloudy quiver over Pairc-na-lee.

By 1919, in "The Second Coming," the Yeatsian apocalyptic symbol has shed its early romance component of the idealized Rose, has lost the starry constellation of the vengeful zodiacal Archer, and, in the hour of its Second Coming, has become "A vision of terror" like the one Yeats saw in the young Maud's soul. Yeats had thought of calling his poem "The Second Birth," but by renaming it "The Second Coming," he ensured that in spite of the rocking cradle, all his recurrences of "mine hour is not yet come" recall the self-manifestation of Jesus not as a child, but as the adult of Cana, the miracle-worker who will return to the world at the end of time.

"The Second Coming" is in fact a thicket of allusions. A hybrid one pointing to Spenser's *The Faerie Queene* and Milton's *Paradise Lost* adds an opaque quality to the mythical dimension of the "rough beast": he cannot be accurately described. Yeats presents him vaguely as "A shape," borrowing from Spenser the concept of Death's resistance to visual representation and from Milton the shapeless word "shape." In Spenser's first Mutabilitie Canto, after a procession of months representing the passage of time, Death, symbol of the end of time, appears both seen and unseeable, "Unbodièd, unsouled, unheard, unseen":

> And after all came *Life*, and lastly *Death*;
> *Death* with most grim and griesly visage seene,
> Yet is he nought but parting of the breath;
> Ne ought to see, but like a shade to weene,
> Vnbodied, vnsoul'd, vnheard, vnseene.

Imitating his master, the "sage and serious poet, Spenser," Milton has his Satan meet Death, equally indescribable except by the word "shape" and its successive ever-less-visible negations (Milton substitutes "shadow" for Spenser's Hades-issued "shade.") Death confounds even Satan:

>   The other shape
> If shape it might be call'd that shape had none
> Distinguishable in member, joynt, or limb,
> Or substance might be call'd that shadow seem'd,
> For each seem'd either; black it stood as Night,
> Fierce as ten Furies, terrible as Hell,
> And shook a dreadful Dart; what seem'd his head
> The likeness of a Kingly Crown had on.

Retaining the word "shape" but changing the concept of the shapeless shadowy "shape" inherited from his predecessors, Yeats attempts to describe in disarticulated images the nameless figure of his own chimerical "vast image" with a "lion body and the head of a man": he adds a description of its gaze "blank and pitiless as the sun," sexualizing it by the "slow thighs" unattached to any completed bodily description, and debasing it by its "slouching" motion, its lurching advance as it gradually reactivates its stony limbs. So grotesque is the figure, so unnameable by any visual word, that Yeats rejects even his own impotent efforts at specialized description, tethering his final question to the vague words "rough beast," offering nothing but its genus. It is a generalized "beast" rather than a recognized species, let alone an individual creature.

THERE ARE, then, four evolving motions successively representing Yeats's mind and emotions in "The Second Coming." We see first an impersonal set of prophetic declamations; these are replaced by a first-person narration of the appearance of the troubling "vast image" coming to replace the Christian past; this, disappearing, is replaced by a "factual" account of the obsolescence of Christianity ("now I know"); but after this flat declaration of secure knowledge, Yeats can muster no further direct object of what he "knows." Instead, he launches a final speculative query ("And what rough beast"). These four feeling-states—impersonal omniscience, a first-person boast of a private "revelation," a "true" historical judgment as to the nightmarish dissolution of the Christian era, and a blurred query uttered in fear—mimic the poet's changes of response as he attempts to write down an accurate poem of this life-moment. A desire for authentically human speech has made him turn away from his initial confident (and baseless) soothsaying to a personal, transitory (and therefore uncertain), private "revelation." He tries finally to attain to truth in judging the end of the Christian era.

But what truth can he declare of what is to come? He acknowledges—in a move wholly unforeseen in the strong and quotable opening octave—how limited his "knowledge" actually is. The "darkness" of fear cannot be resoundingly swept away by a transitory image from an unknowable source: opacity "drops again." By the end,

Yeats must forsake his proposed prophetic and visionary and historical styles and resort to a frustrated human voice that confesses the helplessness of the human intellect and the humiliation of admitting incomplete knowledge. At the inexorable approach of an unknowable, shapeless, coarse, and destructive era, "the darkness drops again."

It is not mistaken, however, to think of the resounding opening summary list as "Yeats's views" as he begins the poem. He even quotes himself in a letter of 1936 to his friend Ethel Mannin, anticipating the next war: "every nerve trembles with horror at what is happening in Europe, 'the ceremony of innocence is drowned.'" The sentiments are genuine, but in a poem something more has to happen than the static observation of a moment in time. A credible artifact has to be constructed, the "sweet sounds" have to be articulated, and a persuasive structure has to be conceived. Since Yeats had lost faith in both Blakean denunciation and Shelleyan optimism by the time he wrote "The Second Coming," he had gained the humility to confess, at the end of the poem, the limits of human knowledge and human vision. Though his diction is still grand in his closing, he is no longer boasting his seer-like knowledge, no longer claiming a unique private vision, no longer able to assuage the nightmare of the End Times of Christianity. To admit Yeats's final acknowledgment of human incapacity is essential to perceiving his overreaching in his earlier claims to prophetic power and visionary insight.

Painful as it is to see the truncated opening lines— however memorable—become all that is left of the poem, and of Yeats's character, in popular understanding, it is more painful to see the disappearance of the human drama of the poem in itself as it evolves, in its desire for authentically human speech and an authentic estimation of human powers—better and truer things than arrogant and stentorian utterances of omniscience. In repudiating his first octave of omniscience, making a break, and then having to write a different "sonnet" to attain a more accurate account of himself and his time, Yeats repeats, by remaking his form, his disavowal of the vain human temptation to prophecy. "Attempting to be more than Man We become less," said Blake, in what could serve as an epigraph to Yeats's intricate and terrifying and regularly misread poem.

The Enigmatical Beauty of
Each Beautiful Enigma

The Bird with the Coppery, Keen Claws

Above the forest of the parakeets,
A parakeet of parakeets prevails,
A pip of life amid a mort of tails.

(The rudiments of tropics are around,
Aloe of ivory, pear of rusty rind.)
His lids are white because his eyes are blind.

He is not paradise of parakeets,
Of his gold ether, golden alguazil,
Except because he broods there and is still.

Panache upon panache, his tails deploy
Upward and outward, in green-vented forms,
His tip a drop of water full of storms.

But though the turbulent tinges undulate
As his pure intellect applies its laws,
He moves not on his coppery, keen claws.

He munches a dry shell while he exerts
His will, yet never ceases, perfect cock,
To flare, in the sun-pallor of his rock.

WALLACE STEVENS

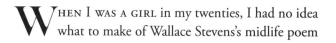

W HEN I WAS A GIRL in my twenties, I had no idea
what to make of Wallace Stevens's midlife poem

"The Bird with the Coppery, Keen Claws." I had come to feel indebted to Stevens's work; I knew there was always a valuable presence inside every poem. But I postponed thinking about "The Bird" because it seemed too surreal, too unrelated to life as I understood it. The birds I knew in verse, from Shakespeare's lark to Keats's swallows, were mostly "real" birds, easily metaphorical birds, flying and singing. Stevens's enigmatic bird, by contrast, was not recognizably drawn from the real thing. The bird is offered as a parakeet, but resembles no real parakeet, if only because he is the "parakeet of parakeets," a Hebrew form of title for a supreme ruler ("King of Kings, Lord of Lords") and because he is characterized, Platonically, as "perfect." I couldn't make sense of the described qualities of the "bird" because they were wholly inconsistent with those of real birds, with those of any imaginable "perfect" bird, and with each other. Stevens's bird (a "he," not an "it") is especially disturbing, because he possesses the powers of intellect and will, powers thought to distinguish human beings from the "lower animals": his "pure intellect" applies its complement of "laws" and he consciously "exerts / His will." And it is only late in the poem that we learn that the bird has intellect and will. What strikes us more immediately is that the bird lacks almost everything we expect in birds: he cannot fly, or see, or mate, or form part of a flock; he remains blind, perched immobile "Above the forest" on "his rock." Put to such puzzlement, I fled, at first, the enigma.

And there was also the problem of the peculiar stanza-form: three five-beat lines per stanza, rhyming in no form I had even seen before—an unrhymed line followed by two lines that rhymed (*abb*). I had seen tercets in Stevens and other poets, but never this kind. In those other tercets, sometimes all three lines would rhyme (*aaa*), or sometimes they would interweave to form Dante's terza rima (*aba*, *bcb*, etc.). There were reasons behind the rhymes—*aaa* becomes emblematic in George Herbert's "Trinity Sunday," and *terza rima* was chosen to point to Dante in Shelley's "The Triumph of Life." But what could be the reason for this strange *abb*? There were *abba* poems, there were *aabb* poems, but there were no *abb* poems. It was an emblem of a lack of something, but of what? I was left guessing about content and form alike. And the stanzas were peculiar in another way: each of the six stopped dead at a terminal period. The reader is instructed, by the insistent conclusive period closing each stanza, to take a full breath between stanzas. Stiffly isolated, stopped after each venture, they did not seem to belong together, nor was there any ongoing narrative to connect them. Most stanzaic poems are more fluid than these representing the bird. Here, one encounters obstruction after obstruction.

"The Bird with the Coppery, Keen Claws" made me ask why a poet would write a poem that seemed unintelligible even to a habitual reader of poetry. Why, I wondered with some resentment, would a poet offer me a poem that presented such obstacles? Only later did I learn that Stevens had said that "the poem must resist the intelligence almost successfully," with the "almost" saving the day by its compliment to the persistent reader. There was, then, work to be done by the reader before the linear string of stanzas could be wound up into a perfect sphere. I knew Blake's promise from *Jerusalem*:

> I give you the end of a golden string,
>   Only wind it into a ball:

It will lead you in at Heavens gate,
Built in Jerusalems wall.

No memorable poem is devoid of art—and the art in the artless is often as difficult to find as the solution of the enigmatic. The "work" of the reader is normally a joyous one; but I was recalcitrant before "The Bird" because I did not yet know how to do the work Stevens expected of me. To be at ease in the poem seemed impossible.

What was the work the poet was demanding of me? It was to inhabit the poem, to live willingly in its world. To do that, one must believe that every word in a poem is, within the poem, literally true, and the first step must be to collect the literal facts from the words. From the title, we know that there is a bird, and the bird has claws. Facts of absence are as important as facts of presence. It is clear that the bird—because he does not sing in the poem—cannot sing, that the bird—because he does not fly in the poem—cannot fly. Although some catastrophe has massacred all the other parakeets of the forest, the parakeet of parakeets has escaped that collective death. Once I understood that I had to take the bird literally, peculiar as that seemed, I became his ornithologist, recording the bird's traits, his present and past habitats, his powers, his hindrances, and his actions.

Stevens's bird strangely possesses an "intellect" and a "will," powers traditionally ascribed solely to human beings precisely in order to differentiate them from "the lower animals." But in spite of his possession of these formidable powers, the bird is strikingly deprived of the actions we most expect in birds: singing and flying. He remains mute, fixed "above the forest" on "his rock." Horribly, he also lacks a bird's keen sight; in a diagnostic logic inferring an inner disease from a bodily deformity, the poet declares dispassionately that "His lids are white because his eyes are blind." "Real" birds, like all organic beings, seek sustenance; they peck for food like the sparrow in Keats's letters, or sip water like George Herbert's birds which "drink, and straight lift up their head." But Stevens's bird is starving, and for lack of anything else feeds on a nutritionless "dry shell" (making it last as long as possible by "munching" it in slow motion). And for Stevens's parakeet there is no mate in this dreadful landscape of parakeet carcasses, this "mort of tails." (The dictionary reveals that the infrequent word "mort" means "a large quantity . . . usually with of," but it also hints, via "mortal," at the French *mort*, "death.") The bird is, in fact, the only "pip" of life remaining in his "paradise." (Keats, in a letter, wrote that "I am . . . sorted to a pip," where "pip" means an ordinary numerical playing card, not a court card.) Although the bird's southern atmosphere, his "gold ether," is indeed paradisal, he, although he is its "alguazil" (a minor Latin American official), cannot be its "golden alguazil," a fit inhabitant of his gold air.

The only thing paradisal about him is that "he broods there and is still," like Milton's Holy Spirit at the opening of *Paradise Lost*, who broods "on the vast abyss." Although the bird is the only living presence (with no rivals as well as no mate or progeny), this exotic creature, despite the gold ether, lives in radically imperfect surroundings. Of possible tropics-yet-to-be, there exist for him only a few unpromising "rudiments": an ivory species of aloe (a succulent that grows in arid soil) and an unappetizing pear with a rind made "rusty" by lethal pear mites. It is doubtful that these "rudiments" can ever again blossom into golden fruit and flowers.

Yet this flightless, blind, and starving bird is—as one continues to encounter his qualities—surprisingly active. The verbs describing his internal motions render them perhaps even superior to flight. He broods in his golden atmosphere, he applies laws with his "pure intellect," he spreads his tails, he munches (even if fruitlessly) on his shell, he exerts his will, and he brilliantly and unceasingly flares ("to display oneself conspicuously," says the dictionary). His flaring outdoes in radiance the sun itself, making the "real" sunlight on his rock seem merely a "sunpallor." The bird's glory lies in his capacity to "deploy," to fan out, his splendid tail-feathers, which undulate in hue—by command of his psychedelic will—in "turbulent tinges." His obscure "tip" is an omen of the future: it is now merely a drop of water but is potentially "full of storms."

Although the bird is externally so immobile, mute, blind, and starved as to seem almost dead, he has begun to experience the feathery stirring of a new creation, in which a generative green turbulence will expand "Upward and outward," populating the desert of carcasses with resurrected golden companions and a regenerated golden self. The powerful golden parakeet-to-be will be able to command, to sing, to see, to fly, to mate, as he did in the paradisal past before all his earlier parakeet-companions were reduced, by some as yet unspecified agent, to a heap of corpses.

STEVENS WRITES such a resistant poem in order, for once, to speak in his "native tongue," to offer not so much an intended communication as a private display. In general, writers want, in at least one work, to express in an unfettered way what it is like to possess a unique mind and speak a unique idiolect (think of *Finnegans Wake* or Raymond Roussel). An unforgettable account of the difficult gestation of such a "resistant" poem can be found in the Romanian Jewish poet Paul Celan's "Es wird," or "Something shall be," which narrates the undertaking and completion of a poem and speculates on its future in posterity. The poet, writing in German, painfully senses within himself an invisible and chaotic residue of excruciating feelings, splintered thoughts, piercing memories, and memorable words—shards of a lost whole broken into pieces by a catastrophe. Celan names the past catastrophe "Wahn," or "madness." Amid the shattered fragments of his former state, the poet rises to the task of creation, of bringing his past whole to life. And his hand, intent on conveying through words the almost unintelligible contour of his broken internal state, brings into a destined proximity the multiple "crazed" fragments of past wholeness, thereby creating on the flat page a hitherto absent unity, the archetypical perfect geometrical form, a circle, symbol of an indisputable completed whole. A circle cannot have parts; it is indivisible, without beginning or end:

Aus dem zerscherbten	Out of shattered
Wahn	madness
steh ich auf	I raise myself
und seh meiner Hand zu,	and watch my hand
wie sie den einen	as it draws the one
einzigen	single
Kreis zieht	circle

But there will be posterity, and Celan prophesies what the perfect silent drawn circle will become when, later, by the alchemy of a reader's thirst, it mutates from its two-dimensional visual form into an unprecedented "something" ("etwas") miraculously aural. From its flat two dimensions that singing "something" will in posterity lift itself into three dimensions, like a fountain, toward a thirsting mouth that will, by a unique reversal of the original silent writing, speak the dead poet's own words aloud in the reader's mouth:

Es wird etwas sein, später,	Something shall be, later,
das füllt sich mit dir	that fills itself with you
und hebt sich	and lifts itself
an einen Mund	to a mouth

To slake our thirst, the circle on the page reforms itself into the mysterious future fountain transmitting the lines on the page into nourishment for us. A life, shattered into fragments, has been reconstituted by the poet's drive to make not a reminiscence of the past but a work of art, a pure geometrical abstraction (Celan's "something"), powerfully satisfying a human reader's insatiable thirst for aesthetic and emotional accuracy.

I must confess that I have presented Celan's stripped poem in narrative order: first the creative assembling under the scribal hand, then (in posterity) a formed refreshment as the reader speaks its sounds. But my narrative order violated Celan's own chosen order: he puts first the poem's astonishing anonymous survival into futurity, and then looks back, now inserting the first-person "I," into his own ecstatic work in creating the impregnable unshattered and unshatterable circle:

Es wird etwas sein, später,	Something shall be, later,
das füllt sich mit dir	that fills itself with you
und hebt sich	and lifts itself
an einen Mund	to a mouth
Aus dem zerscherbten	Out of shattered
Wahn	madness
steh ich auf	I raise myself
und seh meiner Hand zu,	and watch my hand
wie sie den einen	as it draws the one
einzigen	single
Kreis zieht	circle

Celan asks his reader, implicitly, Has my poem not been for you a relief of an unapprehended thirst? Wordsworth conveys a comparable relief in a poignant passage from Book IV of *The Prelude*:

> Strength came where weakness was not known to be,
> At least not felt; and restoration came
> Like an intruder knocking at the door
> Of unacknowledged weariness.

STEVENS's native language in "The Bird with the Coppery, Keen Claws" is one of diction archaic and modern, of unsettling images, of strange assertions, resulting in a startling idiom. Like the language of any poetic style, it can be learned by "foreigners" such as ourselves, and, relieving our demanding thirst, can sound out aloud from our lips. The symbol will re-create the shattered. A poet composing a hermetic poem believes—as Celan here intimates—that posterity, helped by time, will make its sounds "come alive" again.

We can infer, from Stevens's self-portrait as a bird, the crux animating his creation: the shock of having to regard himself in his forties as the survivor of a "madness" of his own. Appalled, he sees that he had been, as a youth, desperately mistaken about himself, his judgment, his marriage, and his aesthetic ideals. His biography—when we look to it—confirms the psychological story of the youth-become-bird. Stevens had to leave Harvard without a degree because his lawyer-father would pay for only three years of schooling—the equivalent of the law school program he himself had followed. The young poet tried ill-paying apprentice journalism, but wanting to marry, he eventually conceded (like both of his brothers) to his father's wishes and went to law school. He encountered no ready success in his first jobs as a lawyer, but nonetheless married (after a five-year courtship conducted mostly in letters) a beautiful girl, Elsie Kachel, to whom he had been introduced in his native Reading.

She had left school at thirteen and, barely educated, was employed to play new pieces on the piano in a music store so that customers would buy the sheet music: Stevens had idealistic dreams of educating her to his own tastes for Emerson and Beethoven. Elsie's parents had married only shortly before her birth, and although her mother remarried after her first husband's death, Elsie was never adopted by her stepfather and retained (as her grave shows) her birth surname Kachel. Stevens's father disapproved of his son's choice of wife, and unforgivably neither parent attended the wedding. Stevens never again spoke to his father or visited the family home until after his father's death; at thirty, he was left fundamentally alone with Elsie. The marriage was an unhappy one, and Elsie, according to their daughter Holly, declined into mental illness. She did not permit visitors to the house, not even children to play with her daughter. Stevens did his entertaining at the Hartford Canoe Club; Elsie gardened and cooked at home. She did not visit her husband during his ten-day dying of cancer in a local hospital.

Several of Stevens's poems reflect both anger and sadness at the failure of the marriage: "Your yes her no, your no her yes" ("Red Loves Kit"); "She can corrode your world, if never you" ("Good Man, Bad Woman"). The poet suppressed many of those lyrics; they did not appear in his *Collected Poems* in 1954. But he left, in "Le Monocle de Mon Oncle," one transparent account of a marriage in which sex has occurred but there has been no meeting of minds or hearts:

> [Love] comes, it blooms, it bears its fruit and dies. . . .
> The laughing sky will see the two of us
> Washed into rinds by rotting winter rains.
> . . . . .
> If sex were all, then every trembling hand
> Could make us squeak, like dolls, the wished-for
>   words.

Humiliating realizations seeped in over the years of the erroneous marriage, eroding Stevens's youthful belief that his thinking was reliable, his personal judgment trustworthy, his aesthetic confidence well-founded, his religious faith solid, and marital happiness attainable. Such a crushing extinction of youthful selves left the poet immobilized in his marriage (he never complained publicly of Elsie, nor contemplated divorce). Starved of sexual or emotional satisfaction at home, working hard at the law, without the company of fellow-artists, unable to sing or soar, brooding in an arid world in which a lost paradise seemed to preclude any domestic hope, Stevens stopped writing poetry (publishing only a few minor pieces) for six years. Although he resumed writing, he did not publish his first book, *Harmonium*, until he was forty-four.

As time went on, Stevens's bitterness became occasionally ungovernable: even the Muse had become deformed and mad. In "Outside of Wedlock," when Stevens is sixty-six, the muse is an unrecognizable Fate:

> The old woman that knocks at the door
> Is not our grandiose destiny.
> It is an old bitch, an old drunk,
> That has been yelling in the dark.

And in 1944, in "This as Including That," a poem of self-address, he lives on a rock and is attended by "The priest of nothingness": "It is true that you live on this rock / And in it. It is wholly you." When at length he exchanged profitless bitterness for stoic resignation, he could, he discovered, still exert intellect and will in a single remaining channel—a hampered but energetic aesthetic expression. Against the "flaring" of beautiful tumultuous undulations Stevens sets the cruel portrait of himself as a bird living on a rock, isolating in his title—of all possible aspects of the bird—only the harsh successive sounds conveying its grating predatory talons, its "Coppery, Keen Claws."

EVENTUALLY I became at home in Stevens's poem and could ask why it took the strange shape I had found so off-putting. The first half of Stevens's self-portrait reproduces a bitterness and hopelessness untranscribable in ordinary language, as he had discovered in trying to write it down literally, jeering (in one suppressed poem) at his youthful romantic mistake with the graffito-title "Red Loves Kit." None of the specific facts of Stevens's life can be deduced from his poetic lines: his discretion and his taste required a departure from any transcriptive candor. Yet this allegorical leaf from a modern bestiary dryly transfuses into the reader the living state of its author—a blind starving bird in a charnel house of former selves who nonetheless has not lost his brooding spirit.

The reader concludes that the massacre of the former forest-parakeets was carried out (since no other agent is mentioned) by their own ruler, the "perfect" parakeet of parakeets, his claws demanding their predatory use. In 1947, almost a quarter-century after "The Bird with Coppery, Keen Claws," the sixty-seven-year-old Stevens, in the sequence "Credences of Summer," bids farewell to the "slaughtered" selves of past infatuations and the raging misleading forces of his springtime. By this self-slaughter of memories and past actions he can even imagine a new fertile Indian summer, created by resuscitated generative flares:

> Now in midsummer come and all fools slaughtered
> And spring's infuriations over and a long way
> To the first autumnal inhalations, young broods
> Are in the grass, the roses are heavy with a weight
> Of fragrance and the mind lays by its trouble.

The parental and marital relationships that had as they occurred seemed so disastrous, causing that "trouble" in the mind, are now seen to be "false disasters," as, in the

eternal return of the seasonal cycle, new energies promise
to resurrect the lost parents and the lost lovers:

> There is nothing more inscribed nor thought nor felt
> And this must comfort the heart's core against
> Its false disasters—these fathers standing round,
> These mothers touching, speaking, being near,
> These lovers waiting in the soft dry grass.

Stevens could not always muster the laying aside of
trouble. Three years later, in "World Without Peculiar-
ity," he rediscovers the very troubles he thought he had
banished:

> The day is great and strong—
> But his father was strong, that lies now
> In the poverty of dirt.
>
> Nothing could be more hushed than the way
> The moon moves toward the night.
> But what his mother was returns and cries on his
>   breast.
>
> The red ripeness of round leaves is thick
> With the spices of red summer.
> But she that he loved turns cold at his light touch.

A few lines later, he gathers together those troubles: they
become "the poverty of dirt, the thing upon his breast, /
The hating woman, the meaningless place." At seventy,
the poet, speaking in ordinary language, can permit him-
self the literal truths that were so impossible to reveal in
1923. The outspoken words—"The hating woman, the
meaningless place"—have become natural only because

he has abandoned the old disasters as false ones: he sees they are in fact only what always happens in the everyday world, disasters not peculiar to oneself but held in common with all mortals.

The tumultuous green undulations of the bird never cease, but they ceaselessly modify their angle of motion. They are produced by the inevitable and necessary fluctuation of the mind in time, "That Which Cannot Be Fixed" (the subtitle of "Two Versions of the Same Poem"). Stevens's bird is so unhappy because he is fixed miserably everywhere in his life except in his plumes. He is a modern and depleted and clawed descendant of Marvell's beautiful bird in "The Garden":

> Casting the body's vest aside,
> My soul into the boughs does glide;
> There like a bird it sits and sings,
> Then whets, and combs its silver wings;
> And, till prepar'd for longer flight,
> Waves in its plumes the various light.

Upward and outward (one could say) Stevens's mythological self-bird waves in its vivid plumes the various light of its pallid sun.

What Stevens had before his eyes at forty-three, as, in his loneliness, he inspected his middle-aged marital and landlocked destiny, was a person immobilized in a life he would never be able to abandon, isolated from his birth-family, unable to see any rewarding emotional future, starved of erotic nourishment and companionship with others, brooding in the spectral company of his past foolish or infuriated selves, looking down at the inert heap of corpses over which he presides, yet still living in the desolate hope of a possible renewed paradise arising from those pitiful rudiments of aloe and pear. That person still possesses intellect and will, knowledge and memory, but is capable, trapped as he is, of interior actions only. Those internal actions awaken sensory, emotional, and intellectual desire: the bird's imagination is still stormy and turbulent, ever capable of infinite creative variations in energy and hue, ever flaring, obedient to his will; in its realm, he exercises his ultimate function, to "flare."

How CAREFULLY, searching for their symbolic counterpart, Stevens tallied each diagnosed deprivation, finding a convincing equivalent of each! One can only imagine the inventive rapture as each of his personal throng of deprivations found its chimerical name, one after another. The whole abjection of a past and present existence lies on the page transformed into words of sharp-featured literalness and self-lacerating implication.

Most poems that touch a reader originate in a pang. (As Stevens said, "One reads poetry with one's nerves.") The pang is the nucleus generating the poet's literal bird. The pang is not "hidden." It is usually—as it is here—in plain view. Inhabit the literal world of this bird who is now you, as you recognize your emotions and write them down: you are immobile and alone, your companions are gone, you lack a mate, you cannot see at all, and you cannot sing. Yet this silent but tumultuous poet is witty in his correspondences: in the world of symbol, metaphor is true; the world is everything that is the case. There is no "hidden meaning": the poem is its own expression of a state of affairs, embodying actuality as its words come alive in our mouths. The poet longs for a depiction of reality as he has known it, and finds that he must resort to representing himself as an enigmatic figure in his own imagined forest, the supreme ruler of nobody. It is the unconcealed chill of the bird, transmitted by its cruelly sonic claws, that convinces us that this parakeet of parakeets slaughtered the fellow-parakeets of his youth when they proved delusory; yet the authorial distance and the cartoon-assemblage of the bird, in its "antic comedy," prevent Stevens's self-portrait from a transcriptive self-pity.

The enigmatical beauty of each beautiful enigma—says Stevens in "An Ordinary Evening in New Haven"—replaces (like Celan's perfect circle) openly revelatory autobiography. In the art of creating and displaying symbolic selves, men willingly lose "That power to conceal they had as men":

> It is as if
> Men turning into things, as comedy,
> Stood, dressed in antic symbols, to display
>
> The truth about themselves, having lost, as things,
> That power to conceal they had as men[.]

As Stevens assembles the shattered fragments of his youthful delusions, he invents the mimetic geometrical form of an "incomplete" three-line stanza, one that can neither make its three lines rhyme nor find a fourth to make the stanza whole. If seeing the bird's plight makes us claim the misery—and self-reproach—in Stevens's words as they become our own, and feel the ever-available cruelty of our own keen claws of intellect and will, and ratify the necessity of our slaughtering the fallacies of youth for authenticity in later life, then we know we have thirsted for the chilly truth welling up as the beautiful enigma unveils its enigmatical beauty. In suppressing his own domestic history, Stevens avoids the misogyny of his complaints in earlier poems: by suppressing Elsie, he assumes sole responsibility for his own condition. When Desdemona is asked who killed her, she says, "Nobody; I myself." The once paradisal, now ugly world of the bird contains no company.

Art and Anger

The Middle-Aged

Their faces, safe as an interior
Of Holland tiles and Oriental carpet,
Where the fruit-bowl, always filled, stood in a light
Of placid afternoon—their voices' measure,
Their figures moving in the Sunday garden
To lay the tea outdoors or trim the borders,
Afflicted, haunted us. For to be young
Was always to live in other peoples' houses
Whose peace, if we sought it, had been made by others,
Was ours at second-hand and not for long.
The custom of the house, not ours, the sun
Fading the silver-blue Fortuny curtains,
The reminiscence of a Christmas party
Of fourteen years ago—all memory,
Signs of possession and of being possessed,
We tasted, tense with envy. They were so kind,
Would have given us anything; the bowl of fruit
Was filled for us, there was a room upstairs
We must call ours: but twenty years of living
They could not give. Nor did they ever speak
Of the coarse stain on that polished balustrade,
The crack in the study window, or the letters
Locked in a drawer and the key destroyed.
All to be understood by us, returning
Late, in our own time—how that peace was made,
Upon what terms, with how much left unsaid.

ADRIENNE RICH

POETRY CAN sometimes offer to the young a piercingly accurate formulation of their inchoate suffering. I remember reading, at twenty-three, two lines in a new book:

> For to be young
> Was always to live in other people's houses[.]

Perhaps some poet had said it before, but if so, I hadn't come across it. I learned from those lines what I was—a provincial girl in a house constituted by persons so alien to me that they were in effect "other people." It had not occurred to me that one could think of one's parents as "other people." It was not "our house"—it was "their house." And where, then, was my house, and how could I find it? And who were my people, if not those in the house with me?

The poem containing those lines was "The Middle-Aged," written in her twenties by Adrienne Rich. It is spoken in the plural "we" by newly adult siblings, as they consider the house in which they grew up—its values, its conditions of "belonging," its rules, its "people." That house of their childhood was established by what the title estrangingly refers to as "The Middle-Aged," the parents now being judged by the altered eyes of their altered young.

When I read those revelatory lines in Rich's second book, *The Diamond Cutters*, I knew almost nothing of her life. I hadn't the slightest notion, before reading her lines, of how to frame the defects—always felt—of my life as a child, but I learned from the lightning bolt of her page that my life was being lived in some other people's house, and they did not understand me, nor I them. Later, reading about Rich's early life (she was born in 1929 and died in 2012), I saw that really we had little in common except that as adolescents we had found ourselves living with people different from us: they were "other people" and we had to live in their house. That formulation— so insistently phrased in the poem—was what Rich so assuagingly offered me. She had "solved," by naming it, the inexplicable misery in which we both had existed as adolescents. We could not speak aloud our disturbingly deep disquiet with the life imposed on us. The problem of a coerced silence was already troubling Rich earlier; her first book, published when she was an undergraduate, had included a poem called "An Unsaid Word," recommending self-suppression in love. She had to train herself not to interrupt the thoughts of "her man," knowing that "this [was] the hardest thing to learn."

The tyranny of the socially unsayable is a pervasive theme in the work of some fiery writers, and the anger provoking their fury often creates, in their verse, problems of tone. In "Easter, 1916," Yeats encounters on the street former friends planning armed revolt against English rule and finds himself betraying a poet's most exigent obligation: to speak intellectual and emotional truth in accurate words. After briefly greeting the conspirators, whose willingness to kill he cannot condone, he bitterly utters first a self-reproach for his cowardice in avoiding truthful conversation, then, using identical words, reproaches himself for actually lingering and prolonging his "meaningless words," an offense worse, because hypocritical, than the first:

> I have passed with a nod of the head
> Or polite meaningless words,

> Or have lingered awhile and said
> Polite meaningless words[.]

Such early self-restriction in fear of social ostracism is likely to result in a later explosion of language. Yeats, for instance, finding "polite meaningless words" intolerable, quite rapidly turned the hitherto unsayable into the complexly said, willing to bear the opprobrium that meets defiance of social norms. Other poets, such as Rich, have a more uncertain evolution within contrary states of feeling.

Rich, conventionally reared, found a relief from self-censorship in discreet poems such as "The Middle-Aged." Like the endangered Hamlet discovering that he must keep silence concerning his father's murder—"But break my heart, for I must hold my tongue"—Rich could not at first become entirely candid about her prolonged suffering (fully revealed to her readers in the recent biography by Hilary Holladay). Her unhappiness—partly situational (an uncongenial family, a failed marriage, social expectations of women), partly physical (as her early rheumatoid arthritis became crippling), and partly uncontrollable (resentment against her father's estrangement from her after she married a Jew)—generated a growing tumult in her work, fortified by a commitment to a newly enthusiastic feminism especially directed against "the patriarchy." After her marriage, Rich found it impossible to hold her tongue as she had done in "The Middle-Aged," and made the search for a responsible tongue a lifelong endeavor.

But like most young protestors, she had on the whole no tolerance for ambiguity, no empathy for opponents, no metaphors for a middle way. If we look back to her chief predecessor in social protest, Milton, we can see him as our most eloquent denouncer of silence in his moving elegy for his fellow-student Edward King (bearing the Greek pastoral name "Lycidas"), who, like Milton, was being trained for the priesthood and already composing poetry. Milton's anonymous surrogate, who sings the elegy for his companion Lycidas, witnesses with horror a flock of local sheep abandoned to hunger and disease by their criminal shepherd-guardians. In a second dereliction of their duty, the guardians have left the sheepfold open to nightly invasion by the "privy paw" of the "grim wolf." Starvation, disease, and massacre meet the innocent eye of the young singer, and his shocked voice reveals the hideous results of the guardians' vices:

> The hungry sheep look up, and are not fed,
> But, swoll'n with wind and the rank mist they draw,
> Rot inwardly, and foul contagion spread;
> Besides what the grim wolf with privy paw
> Daily devours apace . . .

Reacting to that appalling scene of starving sheep and bloody corpses, the singer excoriates the total silence of the bystanders with three bitter words: "and nothing said." The grim wolf every single day, day after day, preys on the hapless sheep, and though everyone witnesses the ghastly daily sight, no one utters a word: the wolf "Daily devours apace, and nothing said." Milton is allegorically rebuking the corrupt English bishops, as the bystanders' fear of episcopal vengeance creates a moral abyss between religious duty and social intimidation. After the young singer's lurid words of denunciation—*swoll'n, rank, rot, foul, grim, devour,* and not least the subhuman *paw* —the accusation arrives, surprisingly, with maximum understatement: "and nothing said." There is no immediate divine vindication of the singer's judgment; the evil shepherds are not punished, not in this poem and not in this life. Only in eternity will they be condemned.

Milton is the principal model for English civic fury, but Rich had other poets in mind as well. The punishment for poetic subversion in Dickinson is banishment, with one's name blackened by rumor. "Don't tell!" she warns any fellow-dissenter. In the Johnson edition, where Rich would have found the poem, it reads:

> I'm Nobody! Who are you?
> Are you – Nobody – Too?
> Then there's a pair of us!
> Don't tell! they'd advertise – you know!

Dickinson's contempt for female social timidity ("Such Dimity Convictions"), however youthfully and lightly voiced in "I'm Nobody," prohibits her from choosing a name from the restrictive role-identities bestowed on women—"Daughter," "Wife," "Mother." She prefers to hide out as "Nobody," defying the parental and institutional assumption that women will take their husband's name after marriage and will fit themselves into some group-identity. (I was struck, on a visit to Dickinson's churchyard in Amherst, by two tombstones, side by side: on the first, two lines identify a man by name and dates, but the neighboring stone says only "His Wife.")

IN THE even-toned blank verse of "The Middle-Aged," Rich, just out of college, ventures her first explicit sally against the dutiful silence expected of her by her parents, equally silent themselves. The reader is made to feel the otherness of parents to their adult children by Rich's strange use of definite articles, beginning in her title. (Normally, we have to acquire the abstract sociological category of "the middle-aged" before we can refer to our parents as merely one set of "the" middle-aged; the title firmly places the parents as permanently sociologically distanced.) As the young adults reflect on their apparently irreproachable parents, their opening vignettes display innocuous adjectives paired with equally innocuous nouns (the parents' "safe" faces, "placid" afternoons, "measured" voices), and continue with comparably "innocent" verbs as the parents "lay the tea" or "trim the borders." Nothing could be less alarming. Yet the verbs immediately following the resuscitated memories are angry and pained: the parents' qualities and behavior—so unoffending, so inoffensive—are to the siblings the very features that they now recoil from, disclosing how "afflicted," how "haunted" they became, as they grew into adolescence, by the stiflingly conventional "custom of the house."

The irreconcilable cohabiting of parental peace and adolescent affliction generates the unforeseen but undeniable aphorism that so disturbed me when I was twenty-three: "For to be young / Was always to live in other people's houses." The "peace" in the house, a tacit agreement by the parents to conceal unlovely marital truths, became unreal to the adult children evaluating it later because it was theirs "at second-hand," an ill-fitting temporary hand-me-down.

The poet insistently disavows the comforts of the parental house even as she names them: the peace, "not ours," the customary life of the house, "not ours." Even the domestic status symbols—the expensive Venetian "silver-blue Fortuny curtains"—have become repellent.

The parents' nostalgic reminiscence of a Christmas party betrays their wish to keep the children children: the parents have to reach back fourteen years to remember the last Christmas party enjoyed by all. Now a second abstract "grown-up" formulation arrives: not only was the house alien in its otherness, but everything about it testified to the ubiquitous parental motive: "Signs of possession" (the upper-class decor) and, more sinisterly for the children, signs "of being possessed." The children are as yet uncritical, essentially owned by the parents who mold their taste: wanting what their parents have amassed, they view their domestic environment "tense with envy." In adulthood, the childhood envy has mutated into hostility.

The rest of the poem undoes the concealments of the house. There is a brief attempt to mitigate the parents' avoidance of candor as Rich recalls the forms of kindness directed at the children: "they" would have given "us" anything, she says—"the bowl of fruit / Was filled for us"; "there was a room upstairs / We must call ours" (we recall the earlier decisive "not ours"). Yet the twenty-year gap separating the generations now produces the "children's" harsh verdict. Against all the apparent parental devotion, Rich instances the persistent scars testifying to secrets never mentioned. The estranging article "the" reappears to present the inscrutability of those mute domestic presences, their unhappy origin never divulged: "the coarse stain," "The crack in the study window," "the letters / Locked in a drawer and the key destroyed." Finally, as the poem closes, the siblings come to understand the artificial "peace" of the house and what was crucially integral to it: "how much [was] left unsaid." "Unsaid"—like Milton's more vehement "and nothing said"—goes on reverberating.

The unsaid continued to preoccupy Rich; her protest against parental authority, suggested rather than nakedly expressed in "The Middle-Aged," turns aggressive in "Tear Gas," a poem she published when she was forty, establishing the parents as cruel enemies:

> Locked in the closet at 4 years old I beat the wall
>   with my body
> that act is in me still[.]

Dickinson made a comparable complaint:

> They shut me up in Prose –
> As when a little Girl
> They put me in the Closet –
> Because they liked me "still" –

Rich's anger against authority mounted to stereotype in some poems of her forties, as it does in the aesthetically untenable "Rape," in which she forgets that a demonic rendering of a fellow human being is rarely persuasive. Here the demon is the neighborhood "cop," who began as a boy you knew: "he comes from your block, grew up with your brothers, / had certain ideals." (The hazy second-person address—"you"—frequent in Rich, exempts the poet from directness: is she addressing herself, the woman in the poem, the reader, or all three?) The "cop" has been brutalized by his own barbaric training, and as the woman reports her rape to him, she notes (or thinks she does) his sexual arousal by her tale; at that point he becomes indistinguishable to her from her rapist. "There is a cop who is both prowler and father," says Rich, improbably opening the poem by intimating that the father of the

reader, too, could become a prowler, since the two iden-
tities are apparently compatible. The woman's perception
that the "cop" is taking pornographic pleasure in her tale
makes her feel raped a second time; she has to "swallow"
his sadistic relishing of the details, as she confesses them,
of the assault. The cop's indecent glistening eyes fuse him
with her rapist. As the poem closes, the woman leaves the
precinct, intimidated and shamed:

> He has access to machinery that could get you put
>   away;
> and if, in the sickening light of the precinct,
> and if, in the sickening light of the precinct,
> your details sound like a portrait of your confessor,
> will you swallow, will you deny them, will you lie
>   your way home?

As the cop becomes her "confessor," he becomes a
Father in the ecclesiastical sense. And who is to say that
the woman's brothers—once, like the cop, guiltless chil-
dren—have not evolved in the same direction as their
boyhood playfellow? Rich widens the stain of rape until
it envelops not only three adult male social roles—father,
sibling, and priest—but also two male criminal roles—
the morally compromised cop, the criminal prowler.

If "Rape" is Rich's moral sermon, her aesthetic sermon
from that violent period of verbal coarseness is the poem
preceding "Rape" in *Diving into the Wreck*: "The Ninth
Symphony of Beethoven Understood at Last as a Sexual
Message." To convey her perception of the music, she
summons up theatrical words: "terror," "howling," "yell-
ing at Joy from the tunnel of the ego," "gagged and bound
and flogged with chords of Joy," "and the / beating of a

bloody fist upon / a splintered table." Not everyone will recognize the symphony in this physically ferocious version. And "Rape" disappoints because in its indignation it sacrifices believability by demonizing generic males in both private and public functions. Although denunciation can be a distinct pleasure, the pleasure it gives is not an aesthetic one. Melodrama, caricature, and stereotyping weaken protest. In any credible poem, whether protest-poem or not, intellectual reflection, social perception, and aesthetic intuition fuse into an imagined entity that does not defy believability.

It takes even great poets some time to come to these virtues of reflective practice. Consider Eliot's early poem called "The Love Song of St. Sebastian," with its unintentional hilarity of rhyme:

> You would love me because I should have strangled
> you
> And because of my infamy;
> And I should love you the more because I had
> mangled you[.]

All indignant poets eventually learn the impotence of a purely oppositional ideology. Milton's Adam comes to understand that the response to evildoing must indeed be acts, but not the Satanic ventures of literal or conceptual war. Rather, as the Archangel Michael tells him, he must add to what he knows,

> Deeds to thy knowledge answerable; add faith,
> Add virtue, patience, temperance; add love,
> By name to come called charity, the soul
> Of all the rest[.]

(Later, under the pretext of a pre-Christian plot, Milton allows physical violence sanctioned by divine "motions" as the blinded Samson kills the Philistines—and himself— by pulling down their temple. Intemperance can recur as temperament reasserts itself.)

IF THE expressive caution of "The Middle-Aged" had to explode into such belligerent poems as "Rape" and "The Ninth Symphony" (both omitted in Rich's *Selected Poems*), Rich eventually found her way to a more finely filtered language of social protest by turning away from polemic absolutes, and by calling on herself and her agitated sympathizers to arrive at "a severer listening, cleansed / of oratory, formulas, choruses, laments, static / crowding the wires." In "Transcendental Etude," dedicated to Michelle Cliff (who became her life-partner), Rich hopes to exhibit "a whole new poetry beginning here," "as if a woman quietly walked away / from the argument and jargon in a room." She begins to assemble for her poetry a nest of varied items from both nature and art, better coinciding with her acknowledgment of her multiple selves: she will write "with no mere will to mastery, / only care for the many-lived, unending / forms in which she finds herself." As she attempted to broaden her lyric repertoire into a globally epic one, her fame grew, and her readings were crowded by hundreds of listeners. Many women found in her work (as I had done as a girl) feelings and situations largely unrepresented in past poetry, but salient in their own domestic and social lives.

Still preoccupied by the pervasiveness of the familial unsaid, however, Rich returned to the topic at fifty-two, writing a new sequence repeating the familial scrutiny undertaken in "The Middle-Aged." "Grandmothers,"

an affecting three-part meditation, names Rich's grand-
mothers in the initial two subtitles of the sequence: first,
her widowed maternal grandmother, Mary Gravely Jones,
an Alabama Episcopalian who visited the Rich family
rarely and formally, all the while "smoldering to the end
with frustrate life," harboring "streams of pent-up words,"
a literary forebear quoting poetry to her grandchildren.
She left behind an unpublished play, but after her mar-
riage gave up writing. Next comes Rich's widowed paternal
grandmother from a New York immigrant Jewish family
who had relocated and prospered in Vicksburg, Missis-
sippi: Hattie Rice Rich is remembered for her "sweetness
of soul," but lacks a home of her own, and is shuttled every
half-year from her son's house to her daughter's house, on
one occasion (recalled by her granddaughter) sobbing at
the imposed transfer. The poet remarks on the paradoxical
life of her grandmother, incapable of living independently
outside an immediate family context: "you had money of
your own but you were homeless." Finally, in the third
poem of the sequence, "Granddaughter," Rich reproaches
herself for her past egotism, for not speculating upon the
inner lives of her grandmothers (fellow females inhabiting
the same house), for not having written "words in which
you might have found / yourselves." The grandmothers—
both widowed, unanchored, untethered, pitiable—had,
at least to their young granddaughter's eye, no life of
their own once their years of wifehood and childrearing
had ended. It is a forlorn poem, its vignettes credible, its
sympathies deep, its self-reproach a surprise after Rich's
earlier presumption of personal righteousness in her most
polemic period.

The quieting of rage is everywhere in the late verse.
(One can even long at times for the excitement and fervor

of Rich's youthful poems.) The self-judgment threaded through the poet's later work does not entirely erase Rich's warm memories of the wild exhilaration of her youth in the city: friends, old neighborhoods, talk, poetry, imagined projects, sex, loud music. But beneath the nostalgic illusory elation lie the graves of that lively company, and the poet's memorial request must be posed to her own hovering death:

> Cut me a skeleton key
> to that other time, that city
> talk starting up, deals and poetry
>
> Tense with elation, exiles
> walking old neighborhoods
> calm journeys of streetcars
>
> revived boldness of cats
> locked eyes of couples
> music playing full blast again
>
> Exhuming the dead   Their questions

Holladay's biography (unfortunately lacking a chronology) tracks the volatile quarrels of Rich's life and verse. The poet's first fierce declaration of independence expended itself on the lifelong quarrel with her autocratic Jewish father Arnold Rich, a brilliant physician and professor, the first Jewish doctor at the Johns Hopkins Medical School. He had extirpated from his family every trace of Jewishness, marrying a gently reared Protestant woman trained as a classical pianist and bringing up his daughters as Episcopalians. In "Sources," a long and absorbing autobiographical poem reflecting on her father's life, Rich addresses their permanent estrangement after her marriage in 1953 to Alfred ("Alf") Conrad (originally Cohen) from an Orthodox Jewish family, a Harvard graduate student in economics (soon promoted to faculty status). No member of either family attended the wedding.

There followed in Rich's life a more open quarrel with political power, pursued together with her husband (who had not been awarded tenure at Harvard) as they moved to New York in 1967, where she taught in Columbia's MFA program as she and Alf both joined the SEEK scheme of alternative education at the City College of New York, where Alf had been appointed chair of the economics department. In this more public form of protest, Rich condemned the inadequacy of government support—for the schools, for the improvement of race relations, for equal justice, for women—and in the SEEK program she taught mostly minority students.

Her increasingly demanding feminism led to a quarrel with marriage itself, as in 1970 she forsook cohabitation with her husband and three sons to live alone in a small New York apartment (while returning each night to cook for the family). Her husband, treated too late for a profound depression, shot himself a few weeks after their separation. The boys returned to Rich's care, and, according to Holladay, remained close to their mother, all visiting her in California as her death approached. Rebelling against her father's wish to erase from his life and his family all remnants of his Jewish origin (which included changing his surname from Reich to Rich and keeping a secular household), Rich began to place more emphasis on her own half-Jewish status, and to recognize the extent of American anti-Semitism.

In her final quarrel with social norms, she wrote about

lesbian sexual experience, and lived with her lesbian part-
ner. Her inner ideological and aesthetic conflicts—visible,
although pent-up, in "The Middle-Aged"—continued
to seek fully formed expression. As she chose to widen
her gaze from those personal conflicts, she undertook
panoramic Whitmanian catalogues of anonymous lives,
aiming—by ranging through space and time—at an epic
"objectivity" rather than subjective self-disclosure. Her
decision is formulated in "And Now":

> I tried to listen to
> the public voice of our time
> tried to survey our public space
> as best I could

Her apologetic tone—"I tried," "as best I could"—marks
her adult sense of her own fallibility and her own limita-
tions as a poet. She also became newly willing (in "The
Spirit of Place") to admit the conflicts struggling to artic-
ulate themselves within the human personality. In New
England, "the spirit of the masters / flickered in the abo-
litionist's heart . . . / while the spirit of the masters / calls
the freedwoman to forget the slave." She concedes that she
and her companions must decline utopian aims and take
on the imperfect world

> as it is   not as we wish it
> as it is   not as we work for it
> to be

Her sermons, increasingly addressed to herself, repent
her earlier wish to control others, and criticize her suscep-
tibility to ideological "counterfeit light":

hold back till the time is right

force nothing, be unforced
accept no giant miracles of growth
by counterfeit light

It is fair to say that the anger exhibited by Rich against all forms of male domination was gradually accompanied by a deep-seated querying of herself. In a poem called "The Phenomenology of Anger," she represents herself as besieged by "Self-hatred, a monotone in the mind," especially as she finds her own rage inextricable from any adult awareness of selfhood, time, and history:

> Every act of becoming conscious
> (it says here in this book)
> is an unnatural act

In "Transcendental Etude," warning against the black-and-white judgments of hasty or unscrutinized anger, she reminds both herself and others who had found themselves seduced by ideological passion that we must "disenthrall ourselves":

>   cleansed
> of oratory, formulas, choruses, laments, static
> crowding the wires.

Like the Polish poet Zbigniew Herbert, who found himself incapable of replicating the clichés of Communist dogma ("fundamentally it was a matter of taste"), Rich came to feel revulsion against the very sound of pre-scripted and prescribed words. In truth it is only a matter of time before a writer who respects the resources of language can no longer echo programmed group-speak, however politically virtuous.

YET NOTHING is harder to sacrifice for a social reformer than the audience-aimed style and psychological reassurance of the doctrinal "we." Even when Rich thinks to abandon the "choral" resonance accompanying the miraculous multiplication of the lonely "I" into the powerful "we," she cannot forsake it, although she alters its extension: her closing "we" in "Transcendental Etude" turns out to be not a sisterly chorus but the fused pronoun of the erotic couple. That idyll, however, cannot wholly compensate for the predicament of "the pitch of utter loneliness" in which each unique poem is "a cry / to which no echo comes or can ever come." Although Rich has claimed the rise of "a whole new poetry" when a woman has "quietly walked away / from the argument and jargon," she discovers that although feeling can be communal and choruses legitimate in pressing for political reform, the only authentic resources for a responsible poet must be her own penetrating imagination and her hard-won idiosyncratic style.

From her early decision in "The Middle-Aged" to expose the unsaid to her later dedication to accurate social reportage and the mitigation of declamatory hyperbole, Rich's poetry records the faithful psychological trajectory of one complicated mind, whose central topic became the sufferings of the subordinated, especially those of women. It must be noted that certain groups of the American subordinated—the blind, the sterile, the impoverished males—did not much interest her. Her political base was always her own smarting social afflictions encountered as a woman, a daughter, a wife, a mother, an exile from her family, a non-observant Jew, a lesbian, a disappointed lover. Her insight into the emotions of others never attained Whitman's spectacular capacity to "effuse" himself into other personalities whose lives were altogether different from his own—a preschool child, an alcoholic, a slave, a soldier. His profound imagination of another's existence justified his unforgettable line, "I am the man, I suffer'd, I was there."

Rich's heated arguments in prose as well as poetry against the coercive customs of her own society brought her fame, chiefly among women, but also led her at times into a regrettable coarseness of expression that she had the courage to abandon in later life, gaining intellectual credibility by a worthy sacrifice of her raised voice. Even as a young poet, Yeats arrived at the realization that "We make out of the quarrel with others, rhetoric, but of the quarrel with ourselves, poetry." Rich made a half-peace with that truth but continued until her death her Whitmanian outward-looking and sometimes vague inventory of suffering, poverty, and needless death in the United States and abroad. Rich's catalogues are in theory unending, and like Whitman's they can sometimes go on too long; they gain plausibility insofar as the items in the inventory embody her specific perceptions of the ubiquity of social failure and the unforeseeable distribution of vice and virtue.

It is not yet clear how Rich will fare in literary history. From her earliest lyric exposures of the unsaid to her later extended investigations of self and society, and from her bracing essays and other prose, she won an audience that was perhaps less attracted by poetic energy than by social critique. (The same could be said of Ginsberg's audience.)

But when the temporary topical relevance of any century's poetry fades, its imaginative and stylistic powers survive. As Stevens says in "Men Made Out of Words," "The whole race is a poet that writes down / The eccentric propositions of its fate."

Strangering

ACCORDING TO Wallace Stevens, "Every poem is a poem within a poem: the poem of the idea within the poem of the words." We often put "the idea" in a brief phrase: "the evils of war." We rarely talk about the poetry of the idea. By itself, the theme, the idea, is always banal: it has to be re-created by the poet's imagination into something animated. (And since the poet at hand is male, I'll call him "he" in what follows.) And then, how is he to arouse a glow of personal vividness within the language, and create "the *poem* of the words"?

Suppose the poet wants the "idea" of his poem to be "the disparity of cultures." What might "the *poem* of the idea" be? This particular poet's imaginative move is to locate his two cultures in cosmic space, on two different planets, one of which is Planet Earth. And how will the words be made into "the *poem* of the words?" An answer occurs to him. What if a visitor from outer space had studied English, but could not escape mistakes in using it for the first time? At this initial stage, there remains a great deal to be done, since both the poem of the idea and the poem of the words are still sketchy and unfulfilled. But at least the poet now has the two poetries to work with. And the poet, Robert Hayden, an Afro-American (his preferred term), is convinced that a poem written by a minority poet has to be as strong in the poetry of its words as in the poetry of its idea. In "Counterpoise," a group manifesto that Hayden published in 1948, he declared emphatically, "as writers who belong to a so-called minority, we are violently opposed to having our work viewed, as the custom is, entirely in the light of sociology and politics."

Let us suppose that it is 1978, and in a new book of poems a reader is seeing an odd entry, bizarrely bracketed fore and aft to show that the title is an editorial addition: "[American Journal]." Who, the reader asks, kept the journal; for whom was it intended; who attached the subsequent title implying, by its non-authorial initial capitals, an editor familiar with written-English usage? The answer is suspended. As the poem opens, the reader sees a series of totally unpunctuated sentiments flowing down the page in hesitant and unequal paragraph-stanzas halted intermittently by pauses. The journal-speaker is fluent, but not error-free, in English. The reader is in fact encountering the internal stream of consciousness of an extraterrestrial, dispatched by his rulers ("The Counselors") to spy on, and report on, a group of brash new planetary invaders calling themselves "americans."

We see that the spaceman has learned only oral English, and knows none of the conventions of written English such as punctuation, apostrophes, and uppercase letters; but there must exist in his own native language some sort of honorific distinction reserved for the rulers, "The Counselors" (the honorific is translated in his journal by its sole and singular use of capital letters). In the poem's prologue, the extraterrestrial muses on his new situation:

here among them   the americans   this baffling
multi people   extremes and variegations   their
noise   restlessness   their almost frightening
energy   how best describe these aliens in my
reports to The Counselors

disguise myself in order to study them unobserved
adapting their varied pigmentations   white black
red brown yellow   the imprecise and strangering
distinctions by which they live   by which they
justify their cruelties to one another

charming savages   enlightened primitives   brash
new comers lately sprung up in our galaxy   how
describe them   do they indeed know what or who
they are   do not seem to   yet no other beings
in the universe make more extravagant claims
for their importance and identity

The spy, disguised and passing as a fellow-citizen, stud-
ies the unfamiliar new tribe, noting its heterogeneity, its
"strangering" distinctions, and its repellent moral justi-
fications. Little by little the inner voice of the spy reveals
his burden: he must compose a report for The Counselors,
and he feels inadequate to the task. Although the planet
of the "aliens" belongs to the same galaxy as his own, he
knows no group in the entire universe who regard them-
selves so insolently, so proudly, as these "savages" do. So far,
the extraterrestrial voice has offered relatively little infor-
mation about its own powers and intentions; only later—
during a visit to a rough tavern—does it reveal that it has
masked itself (at least in the tavern) as male. I am calling
the voice "he," but it has the power to exist in different
genders and can adopt local skin-pigmentation at will.

    Since the planetary visitor is addressing himself, we can
only guess, from his own categories and judgments, what
sort of person is generating these words. We learn that he
is frightened by lawless energy, by noise, by unpredict-
able restlessness, by multiple skin-colors: in disguise he

has "adapted"—but he means "adopted"—various pig-
mentations depending on his social context. "Adapted" is
one of his linguistic falterings, like "strangering" (in lieu
of "strange"). He has strong moral views and is revolted
by the cruelties he sees among these "savages" (however
charming); he has equally strong intellectual views, judg-
ing the newcomers as "primitives" (however sophisticated
their technology). To him, the "americans" are aliens inca-
pable of introspection or self-analysis yet ever boastful in
their claims to importance and to a unique identity.

HAYDEN'S 115-LINE "[American Journal]" has attracted a
good deal of contemporary attention, but its imaginative
swirls of inconsistent "american" ideologies and behaviors
have provoked more critical observation than its equally
imaginative flights of language. I want to reflect here on
Hayden's imaginative interest in creating a spaceman's
mind and forms of expression. "The Counselors" on the
spaceman's planet apparently maintain a training labora-
tory for spies, providing language-tapes of any culture they
intend to investigate. Two sets of these tapes are labeled
"English," one transmitting British English and the other
American English, and the spy has been afforded both
sets for his diligent preparatory study. One of the most
entertaining aspects of this nonetheless serious poem is its
presentation of the verbal and interpretive blunders that
any visitor to a foreign land is bound to commit when he
finds himself embedded in a bewildering unknown cul-
ture. Hayden must have taken intense pleasure in think-
ing up, all through, the multifaceted "poem of the words"
used by the alien.

"[American Journal]" presents itself as a quasi-

symphonic poem, advancing with the fluidity of musi-
cal movements in the spaceman's successive choices of
aspect: scenes, emotions, distinctions of pacing, degree
of self-distancing. After the opening prologue, the voice
(perhaps to reassure The Counselors) begins to liken this
brash new species to his own tribe; "like us," he says, they
have advanced technology and have traveled to the moon
(grossly leaving their "rubbish" behind); and apparently
they too worship "the Unknowable Essence" (but how do
they define their Unknowable?). In lieu of shamans they
have "technologists" (a native speaker might have said
"scientists"). The observer tallies geographical and mete-
orological Earth features that he recognizes from his own
home-planet, including the temporal feature of the sun by
day, the moon by night:

> oceans deserts mountains grain fields canyons
> forest   variousness of landscapes weathers
> sun light moon light as at home

Nostalgia for "home" has made him begin his obser-
vations with familiar perceptions, but he is as yet a novice
in English pronunciation: he separates the word "sun"
from "light" and "moon" from "light," as though his over-
arching category "light" has separate subordinate catego-
ries, that of the sun and that of the moon. With him, the
light has not, as in native English voicing, been absorbed
almost silently into the polysyllabic "moonlight" and
"sunlight."

The observer, we are pleased to see, has an aesthetic
sense resembling our own, responding instantly to "red
monoliths" like those of his remembered "home":

>   much here is
> beautiful   dream like vistas reminding me of
> home   item   have seen the rock place known
> as garden of the gods and sacred to the first
> indigenes   red monoliths of home

For the first time, an actual American name has at this point made its way into the spaceman's report: the so-called Garden of the Gods in Colorado Springs is a stark terrain of red monoliths held sacred by Native Americans. The name points us to an incident in the life of Robert Hayden. In 1975, five years before his death, the day after his reading at Colorado College, Hayden visited the Garden of the Gods at the invitation of a young MFA student whom he had met the night before. A few years afterwards, that student—Yusef Komunyakaa, later a distinguished poet himself—recorded their walk:

> Hayden had to be assisted closely along the rocky paths up the beautiful hills. He seemed nearly blind. . . . Soon we were in the heart of the Garden of the Gods, beside a formation called Balanced Rock—a smaller stone supporting a larger one, massively depicting a visual mathematics too subtle for words. Hayden stopped, looked around, and said, "I love this country."

In "[American Journal]" Hayden bestows his own warm response to the grandeur of the scene on his extraterrestrial, fusing himself and the surreal cosmic visitor.

A reader aware that Hayden is African American may suspect that he is satirizing, in the response of the technically sophisticated alien contemplating the americans,

the discourse of a "civilized" white gazing, with simul-
taneous denigration and envy, at a "primitive" Black
culture. But by now enough ink has been spent on the
poem to discourage any idea that its "message" is without
subtlety; a number of identity-determinants—national,
linguistic, gendered—populate the poem. Although the
spy celebrates the landscape so like his own, he is not
free to mention in his report the sensuous appeal of the
americans themselves. After his search for the right adjec-
tive to describe them—"i am attracted to / the vigorous
americans   disturbing sensuous"—he becomes ashamed,
adding "never to be admitted," meaning, surely, not even
to himself.

The next movement of the poem is a scherzo, in which
the alien-in-disguise has a conversation in a tavern with an
American. When he asks what is meant by "the american
dream" the "earth man" answers in ignorant colloquial
language (with its crude "irregardless," its unthinking alli-
ance of "sure" and "i guess"). The alien, never having read
written English, is mistaken in substituting two words for
the proper English single word, as in "night mare" and
"every body"), and he is baffled by the redundant inser-
tion of the all-purpose American linguistic filler, "okay."
The earth man says, of the american dream:

                                                                sure

we still believe in it i guess . . .

                              irregardless of the some
times night mare facts we always try to double
talk our way around   and its okay the dreams
okay and means whats good could be a damn sight
better   means every body in the good old u s a

> should have the chance to get ahead or at least
> should have three squares a day   as for myself
> i do okay   not crying hunger with a loaf of
> bread tucked under my arm you understand

The alien's dutiful previous listening to the tapes of spoken English does not equip him to understand the torrent of incorrectness, slang ("double talk," "three squares"), and abbreviations ("u s a") uttered by the earth man. He puts forth, in reply to this barrage of American dialect, his courteous British reply (deriving from his alternate set of language-tapes, the British one): "i / fear one does not clearly follow." His tavern-mate becomes suspicious:

> notice you got a funny accent pal   like where
> you from he asked   far from here i mumbled
> he stared hard   i left

The tavern-dialogue teaches the alien that his linguistic mimicry is still imperfect:

> must be more careful   item   learn to use okay
> their pass word   okay

After the comic interlude of the tavern scene, however, "[American Journal]" suddenly turns savage, as a street riot erupts, alive with new unintelligibility. The alien sees people he characterizes as "sentinels"—a literal translation from some word in his native tongue, since he hasn't learned the correct English word for "police." The "sentinels" are disturbingly recharacterized by the crowd—"pigs / i heard them called"—as the police retaliate "with flailing clubs":

> unbearable decibels   i fled lest
> vibrations of the brutal scene do further harm
> to my metabolism already over taxed

A biological fact about the alien—that under the rule of The Counselors the capacity to tolerate violence has been genetically bred out of his metabolism—leads him to side with the police, as with the primary authoritarian decisions that have created and socialized him. His voice becomes that of a repressed creature unconscious of his own victimization, incapable until now of any mental act not channeling the opinions of The Counselors. Yet his equilibrium has been so shaken by the violence of the riot that the very word "serenity" shatters into linguistic fragments over a line-ending:

> The Counselors would never permit such barbarous
> confusion   they know what is best for our sereni
> ty   we are an ancient race and have outgrown
> illusions cherished here   item   their vaunted
> liberty

His (temporary) identification with The Counselors allows the alien to parody the earth-men's truculence:

> no body pushes me around i have heard
> them say   land of the free they sing   what do
> they fear mistrust betray more than the freedom
> they boast of in their ignorant pride   have seen
> the squalid ghettoes in their violent cities

(Nowhere does the alien sound more like a white suprem-acist than here: he has learned, and uses, the abusive word "ghettoes.") And he wonders, returning to the word "paradox" from an earlier summary:

> paradox on paradox   how have the americans
> managed to survive

After the deafening street riot there arrives a louder scherzo than the earlier tavern-interlude: now it is the "patriotic" spectacle of the Fourth of July. As "earth men / in antique uniforms play at the carnage whereby / the americans achieved identity," the alien reveals that on his own planet they indeed do study American history in its origins:

> we too recall
> that struggle as enterprise of suffering and
> faith uniquely theirs

But what has happened in the vulgar modern era to the noble independence celebrated on the Fourth? With mockery the alien sees its debasement into a craven nationalism:

> blonde miss teen age
> America waving from a red white and blue flower
> float as the goddess of liberty   a divided
> people seeking reassurance from a past few under
> stand and many scorn

"A past [that] few under / stand and many scorn": in these high-minded words the alien exhibits his own superior wisdom as he judges American ignorance and political decline. And hearing contemporary skeptics dismiss the Fourth of July parade ("why should we sanction / old hypocrisies"), the alien returns to his "native" moralizing and irritated scorn. Yet his anxiety exhibits itself afresh as the revered word "Counselors" breaks into pieces at a line end:

> The Counse
> lors would silence them
>
> a decadent people The Counselors believe   i
> do not find them decadent   a refutation not
> permitted me

The Counselors, we begin to understand, do not countenance objections to their views. The alien's irrepressible mixed feelings about the Americans throw him into a violent mixed diction as he ends up siding with The Counselors' stereotypes of "raw crude" "earthlings":

> but for all their knowledge
> power and inventiveness not yet more than raw
> crude neophytes like earthlings everywhere

With the subsiding of his unresolved responses to the Fourth of July, the alien wonders how his report on America will strike The Counselors. Since he is, himself, delighted by the ingenuity of his multiple disguises, he reminds himself *sotto voce* to induce approval in The Counselors by describing his stratagems. But even while reassuring himself that The Counselors will admire his powers, he still worries about their eventual estimation of his work. Hoping to curry favor, he describes his spy-costumes in a cascade of nouns and idioms learned, we feel, rather on the street than from the bland tapes of his language-lab:

though i have easily passed for an american   in
bankers grey afro and dashiki long hair and jeans
hard hat yarmulke mini skirt   describe in some
detail for the amusement of The Counselors   and
though my skill in mimicry is impeccable   as
indeed The Counselors are aware   some thing
eludes me   some constant amid the variables
defies analysis and imitation   will i be judged
incompetent

In his next, most analytical moment, the extraterrestrial
rises to the philosophical diction natural to his culture—a
discourse technologically supreme, wholly rational, but
emotionally repressed. The minor role of America in the
cosmic scheme of things ("an iota in our / galaxy") is evi-
dent to him, but he is disturbed by its problematic exis-
tence as a conceptually insoluble entity, resistant—in its
mobile lability of science and fantasy, logic, and imagina-
tion—to the analytic reason that is the pride of his civili-
zation. He sighs in frustration:

america   as much a problem in metaphysics as
it is a nation earthly entity an iota in our
galaxy   an organism that changes even as i
examine it   fact and fantasy never twice the
same   so many variables

As the spy ponders the unintelligibility of America,
its antagonism to all he has valued, he realizes that he is
in physical danger from its natives: already his presence
has been rumored in the newspapers. While the papers
laugh at those "believing" in the existence of "human-
oids," the "humanoids" in their spaceship laugh back at

the scoffing newspapers. Quiet in his withdrawal from the company of his "crew," the alien reflects on all he has seen and heard: the gaudy Fourth of July parade, "blonde miss teen age America," the suspicious earth man in the tavern, the street-riot between citizens and "sentinels," the awful decibels of both celebration and violence, the confluence in the streets of dashikis and yarmulkes. Lost in his memories, the alien, tensely frustrated, cannot define what the Americans are: he knows only that the American personality confounds his own schooled, careful, sexless, logical self. He cannot, now, return unthinkingly to his own sterile planet, submit to The Counselors' rules, and censor his speech. Once home, he will ponder the "variegations" of his past journey—his adroit disguises of body, skin-color, gender, and manner of speech—but for all his wide-ranging observation, he will remain forever unable to solve the "quiddity"—the "thisness"—of this paradoxical population, this exuberant and savage rebel-tribe.

HAYDEN'S SCIENCE fiction is doubly dystopian. His spacemen are like Swift's whinnying Houyhnhnms, inhuman, chilly, fastidious, rational; and their representative courier flinches at the Americans' untidiness, their boasting, their costumed mimicry of the carnage of 1776, their cruelty, their childish "floats," their veneration of the "goddess of liberty" in the person of a teenager in a toga, their incoherent "metaphysics," their elusive essence.

Behind the agitated monologue of the visiting "humanoid" lies the implied story of his former life: he was born, he was schooled, he was reprimanded for any excess of act or emotion, he was indistinguishable from others of his tribe. Passionless, he needed no human relations (family, wife, children); he worshipped "technologists," and excelled in scientific observation, memory, and analysis. Posted to another planet to spy on the brash new tribe of "earthlings," he is disposed at first to dismiss their childish "civilization," but eventually, as he moves among them, he discovers in their "varied" pigments and "various" behaviors much that he has lacked in his artificially rational former life. And what will his future be? He will be sadder, and wiser, forever alienated from his compliant fellow-citizens, unable to convey to them the extravagance of emotion and action, free from punitive supervision, that the Americans, for all their faults, possess.

Hayden made room in his poem for his extraterrestrial's implied past and presumably alienated future to sharpen the contrast of the two cultures, the governed rational and the unbridled free. Both are insufficient, both are incomplete. The rational and disciplined one sees the unbridled one as ungovernable; the unbridled one would see the alien's authoritarian Counselors as intolerable. Neither culture is really admirable. The chief difference between them is that one is subjugated, the other free (in both virtue and vulgarity). The free culture has no stable government; its people are unruly, as likely to sponsor a riot as a parade. The governed culture has the dark stability of its euphemized "counseling"—coercive, repressive, severe, implacable.

Hayden invented from scratch the unusual sensibility and the "faulty" English of the alien, his innocence as to punctuation and spelling, his nervousness intermittently betrayed by his words' falling into pieces (not syllables), his complacent moral judgments, his intellectual scorn of the "earthlings" who have gotten to the moon but no farther, his horror at the sheer noise of the American streets in parades and riots—all the while showing his opinions being put into question by that elusive "something" for which he has no words. It is, of course, freedom, both in creation and in destruction.

We can, if we choose, read this conflict of cultures as embodying on the one side technologically schooled and hierarchically socialized America and on the other side that supercilious America's view of African American life. There is something to that reading, but not everything. Hayden repudiated the narration of victimhood as the chief resource of a minority writer, just as he repudiated despair at the racial division of his America. His "God-consciousness" (as he named it) led him to an unshakeable conviction of human brotherhood and enabled him ultimately to join his wife Erma's church, the Baha'i, which exists without a hierarchical structure and affirms belief in the unity of all humankind.

And yet Hayden had, by his own acknowledgment, periods of profound depression as well as periods of strenuous belief that relations between the races could not only improve but become harmonious. He incurred the wrath of the Black Power movement in the 1970s because of his conviction that the literature of organized protest movements tended toward propaganda, not art. Nor could he bring himself to refuse Emersonian symbolism in favor of literal statement. When an interviewer asked him why he wrote poetry, he said—disarmingly and wittily—because he liked it better than prose. He thought "confessional" poetry too naked to attain universality. He never stopped revising his poems in the direction of greater concision, greater symbolic power, and greater objectivity. Famous for his powerful sequences of African American history—"Middle Passage," "John Brown"—he is justly remembered in most anthologies for the inexpressibly moving "Those Winter Sundays," an elegy for his laborer foster-father. "Sundays too my father got up early," it begins, with all the emphasis on the accented "too": "got up early" as a kindness to the sleeping family in the cold house, making "banked fires blaze." "No one ever thanked him": that is the line of the poem that no one can ever forget.

Once Hayden learned to read—by himself, at three— he read intensely and passionately the major British and American poets. One can see him, over a lifetime, experimenting with nearly all poetic genres: nature lyrics, elegies, sequences, allegories, ballads. When he looked to African American predecessors, he saw some of them writing in dialect, others creating new folk ballads, still others choosing the high language of the canonical English lyric. He would learn from them, but equally from Whitman, Crane, and Auden (who taught Hayden at Michigan). Just as Elizabeth Bishop would not allow her poems to appear in single-gender anthologies because she took herself to be an American poet, not a "female poet," so Hayden always believed himself to be an American poet among other American poets. For him, the democracy of literature could not countenance partisan hostilities, nor could the brotherhood of human beings conceive of exclusions within the company of artists.

Born in Detroit in 1913 and named Asa Sheffley by his birth-parents, the poet was given away, but not abandoned, by his mother when she moved to find work. He was raised (but never adopted) by a neighborhood family, the Haydens, and subsequently went by the name Robert Hayden. He came to feel that his foster-family meant well by him; his father did not obstruct his intellectual desires, and saved to help him through college, but it was a teacher, a librarian, and a social worker (assigned to the Haydens when they were on welfare) who saw something unusual in him and encouraged him. In his prose, he was candid about his group difficulties in school; with his thick glasses, his poor sight, and his love of poetry, he was called "Nigger. Four-Eyes, sissy." In view of the violent racial divisions of American life, which he experienced from childhood with unavoidable pain, he thought that an artist had to cultivate a strict objectivity in social observation. He supported himself all his life by teaching. For twenty years he remained at Fisk (teaching fifteen hours a week, a taxing load for a conscientious teacher), and thereafter he closed his career at the University of Michigan. In 1976, the Bicentennial Year, he was appointed Consultant in Poetry to the Library of Congress (a congratulatory post now renamed, more accurately, Poet Laureate). The final triumph of Hayden's personal and impersonal objectivity was "[American Journal]," composed in 1976 as the Phi Beta Kappa poem for the University of Michigan and placed as the final work in his *Collected Poems*. You can hear Hayden read it in his quiet and musical voice on a tape he made for the Library of Congress in 1978, two years before he died, early, at 66, of cancer.

Art Against Stereotype

England

with its baby rivers and little towns, each with its abbey or its
                              cathedral,
     with voices—one voice perhaps, echoing through the transept—the
criterion of suitability and convenience: and Italy with its equal
          shores—contriving an epicureanism from which the grossness
                              has been

extracted: and Greece with its goats and its gourds, the nest of
                              modified illusions:
     and France, the "chrysalis of the nocturnal butterfly" in
whose products, mystery of construction diverts one from what
                              was originally one's
          object—substance at the core: and the East with its snails,
                              its emotional

shorthand and jade cockroaches, its rock crystal and its
                              imperturbability,
     all of museum quality: and America where there
is the little old ramshackle victoria in the south, where cigars are
                              smoked on the
          street in the north; where there are no proofreaders, no
                              silkworms, no digressions;

the wild man's land; grass-less, links-less, language-less country
                              in which letters are written
     not in Spanish, not in Greek, not in Latin, not in shorthand
but in plain American which cats and dogs can read! The letter "a"
                              in psalm and calm when
          pronounced with the sound of "a" in candle, is very noticeable
                              but

why should continents of misapprehension have to be accounted for
by the
fact? Does it follow that because there are poisonous toadstools
which resemble mushrooms, both are dangerous? In the case of
mettlesomeness which may be
mistaken for appetite, of heat which may appear to be haste,
no con-

clusions may be drawn. To have misapprehended the matter, is to
have confessed
that one has not looked far enough. The sublimated wisdom
of China, Egyptian discernment, the cataclysmic torrent of emotion
compressed
in the verbs of the Hebrew language, the books of the man
who is able

to say, "I envy nobody but him and him only, who catches more
fish than
I do,"—the flower and fruit of all that noted superi-
ority—should one not have stumbled upon it in America, must
one imagine
that it is not there? It has never been confined to one locality.

MARIANNE MOORE

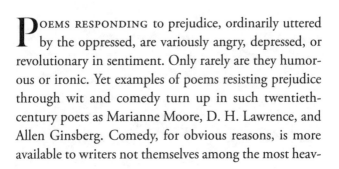

POEMS RESPONDING to prejudice, ordinarily uttered
by the oppressed, are variously angry, depressed, or
revolutionary in sentiment. Only rarely are they humor-
ous or ironic. Yet examples of poems resisting prejudice
through wit and comedy turn up in such twentieth-
century poets as Marianne Moore, D. H. Lawrence, and
Allen Ginsberg. Comedy, for obvious reasons, is more
available to writers not themselves among the most heav-

ily oppressed; although they may belong to oppressed populations (women, the Welsh, homosexuals), they have usually become—through innate genius, childhood wealth, or admission to elite education—socially equal (or superior) to their earlier oppressors.

Marianne Moore, for example, was born to the daughter of a well-off Presbyterian minister, but also to a psychotic father confined in an asylum. She and her mother were relatively impoverished after her grandfather's death when she was seven. Yet she was educated at Bryn Mawr, and became after college a teacher "of English and business subjects" (at one of the now-infamous boarding schools for "Indians"), a librarian, and the editor of an avant-garde journal. She also had the luck of having her poems brought to the attention of T. S. Eliot in England through the influence of her poet-friend Hilda Doolittle (whose wealthy lover, Winifred Ellerman, paid for the original publication of Moore's poems in England without Moore's knowledge or consent).

Although Moore was trained in college to recognize social prejudice—she enthusiastically attended lectures by visiting feminists at Bryn Mawr and took an interest in the Suffragist movement—she was also, I think, brought up by her mother (who eventually took a lesbian lover) to feel indignant at the common private prejudice against those who, like herself later, resisted the usual social program of female life. (Emily Dickinson, even more eccentric than Moore, had implicitly described herself to Thomas Wentworth Higginson as of a different species from conventional women: "the only Kangaroo among the Beauty.") When Moore visited England in 1911 with her mother, she was nettled by the persistent prejudice there against all things American; and in 1920, in a poem mischievously titled "England," she could afford (because of her maternal family and her upper-class education) to choose satire rather than resentment as her initial weapon against hostile English judgments of things American. In between a scanty overture on England and a coda on America, Moore recites common stereotypes of Italy, Greece, France, and "the East" before coming to a defiant conclusion which not only counters English prejudice against America, but also confesses to her own previously unconscious use of superficial stereotypes.

Moore's chief precursors in asserting America's right to contest the Old World's supposed excellence were Whitman and Dickinson. In 1871, by invitation, Whitman recited "Song of the Exposition" at the fortieth National Industrial Exposition in New York City, sponsored to display the newest products of agriculture and machinery. In the poem, he blithely disdains the assumed superiority of the European classics, flippantly declaring to the Muse that she has exhausted the literary materials of the past. Urging her to join him in the New World, he is irresistibly persuasive:

> Come Muse migrate from Greece and Ionia,
> Cross out please those immensely overpaid accounts,
> That matter of Troy and Achilles' wrath, and Æneas',
>   Odysseus' wanderings,
> Placard "Removed" and "To Let" on the rocks of
>   your snowy Parnassus . . .
> For know a better, fresher, busier sphere, a wide,
>   untried domain awaits, demands you.

Predicting the Muse's smiling response to his call, he

announces to his fellow citizens her choice of location for her new American shrine:

> Bluff'd not a bit by drain-pipe, gasometers, artificial
>   fertilizers,
> Smiling and pleas'd with palpable intent to stay,
> She's here, install'd amid the kitchen ware!

Dickinson, for her part, mocked the adoption by New England women of English manners and complacent class-consciousness, reproaching her contemporaries' supposed "Convictions" as ones composed of "Dimity" (a light summer cotton dress-fabric) and their Christianity as one that would haughtily recoil from St. Peter himself as a mere "Fisherman":

> Such Dimity Convictions –
> A Horror so refined
> Of freckled Human Nature –
> Of Deity – Ashamed –
>
> It's such a common – Glory –
> A Fisherman's – Degree –

Most nineteenth-century American poets—contemporaries of the scandalous Whitman and the unknown Dickinson—had tended to imitate beloved English models (while substituting American heroes or locales for English ones). Longfellow, Bryant, Whittier, and Lowell wrote in all the conventional genres: accomplished ballads, seasonal observations, philosophical reflections, elegies, love lyrics, satires, hymns. But Whitman and Dickinson—already social exiles but superbly self-educated—broke the Anglophone molds of subject and form, and so did the subsequent American modernists, Moore among them.

Conscious of herself as a misfit, Moore deliberately wrote poems about misfits, sometimes exotic untamed animals (an ostrich, a giraffe) and sometimes handicapped vegetables (a carrot thwarted of its genetic shape by natural obstructions, a strawberry distorted in shape by a struggle in growth). The most piercing—because the most personal—of her misfits is a tree. "The Monkey Puzzler," which appeared in 1925 in the second edition of her first American publication, the vividly original *Observations,* describes a bizarre species of Chilean pine putting forth spiky branches which, instead of spreading out, curl back on themselves. Perhaps owing to her own Irish forebears—"I am troubled, I'm dissatisfied, I'm Irish"— Moore was drawn to the half-Irish, half-Greek [Patrick] Lafcadio Hearn, another misfit in both Dublin and the United States, who eventually took Japan as his country. Moore quotes his praise of the monkey puzzle tree's peculiar aesthetic appeal:

> This porcupine-quilled, infinitely complicated
>   starkness—
> this is beauty—"a certain proportion in the skeleton
>   which gives the best results."

But praise does not solve the questions that a naturalist would ask of the monkey puzzle tree: How did it come to originate in Chile? And how was it genetically compelled into its strange distortions? One cannot answer such questions, any more than one can account for nature's casting an idiosyncratic human child of linguistic genius into a strained Missouri ecclesiastical environment. Moore, knowing her own eccentricity, closes her impersonal third-person portrait of the monkey puzzle tree with a human first-person "we"—a strikingly pained but accurate self-recognition. At the last moment she discovers a new verb ("prove") of self-justification:

> One is at a loss, however, to know why it should
> be here,
> in this morose part of the earth—
> to account for its origin at all;
> but we prove, we do not explain our birth.

How did a Missouri girl born of a domineering mother and a psychotic engineer-father (whom she never knew) become a poet? Why in her adult life did she remain unmarried, living (except for her four years at Bryn Mawr) in rented apartments with her mother, sharing her bed until she was fifty-nine, and later buried with her under a joint tombstone? Her sole testimony to her individual existence was the poetry that she generated: "we prove, we do not explain our birth." The climactic "prove" (from the Latin *probare,* "to test") shines out in all its plural meanings: we prove our life has a purpose; we test the value of our birth; we dare to exhibit to others our strangeness-from-birth; we claim a right to our birth-identity by the proof of its creations.

MANY OF Moore's poems are about such oddities as the monkey puzzle tree. For her, such strange things derive their intrinsic value from their creation by God. Brought up through her seventh year in the house of her Presbyterian minister-grandfather, daughter to her religious mother, and sister to her Presbyterian minister-brother,

Moore (with and like her mother) remained a church-going Christian. Myth and nature appear in her poetry as rich sources of the eccentric: unicorns, dragons, pango-lins, the plumet basilisk, the jerboa, the octopus, the por-cupine—these caught her eye, all of them animals never domesticated. In "Black Earth," a glorious self-portrait where she speaks in the first person as an elephant in the wild, she is represented as entirely free. She remained psychologically undomesticated herself, in spite of her never-terminated maternal connection and the strong family ties generating countless interwoven letters among her mother, her brother, and herself, in which each went by the name of an ungendered and undomesticated ani-mal: "Rat" was Marianne, "Mole" was her mother Mary (sometimes called by other animal names such as "Fawn" or "Cub"), and "Badger" was her elder brother John. The family group seemed to others essentially impenetrable. Mary, who had become an English teacher, set the linguis-tic standard which her daughter—though always defer-ring to the example of her mother—far surpassed.

A restless reader both in conventional subjects (litera-ture, history, mythology, art) and in odd corners of exotica (the outliers of the animal kingdom, anthropology, cou-turier fashions, geography), Moore dared to envisage an audience as extravagantly informed as herself. Her stanzas elaborate themselves by inlaid bits and pieces, relics of the intellectual accumulation of a lifelong collector of the remote and the strange. In almost every poem, ecological and historical and aesthetic details crowd together in what seems a forbidding hedge between her pages and any ill-read reader. She understands, from her new acquaintance with England, that the English regard America as a misfit among countries, a savage land alien to Anglo-European "civilization," with "inferior" mores and manners. In "England," she will comically teach our transatlantic relatives otherwise.

"ENGLAND"—ITS TITLE spilling over into its descriptions—seems to begin innocently enough, with touristic stereotypes of England's geography and its Christianity:

England

with its baby rivers and little towns, each with its abbey or its
                    cathedral,
   with voices—one voice perhaps, echoing through
                    the transept—the
criterion of suitability and convenience . . .

This description seems initially bland enough to be included in a travel brochure, but Moore's first insidious gesture—voiced by a critical sensibility foreign to England—is to slip in the tiny adjective "baby." Who would call English streams—the Thames, the Wye —"baby rivers," except someone who knew the broad Mississippi or another "giant" river of the Americas? Who, except one who had taken the measure of New York or Chicago, would see all English towns as "little" and tediously identical in their monocultural Christianity except that one has an abbey, another a cathedral? Who—knowing choral possibilities—would limit a cathedral transept to "one voice perhaps," the most minimal musical requirement? And who, familiar with the mighty ambitions of European Christian music, would regard the anorexic English criterion of "suitability and convenience" as sufficient for a whole country? It is an

American voice, with its own contempt for a declining England of limited ambition, that utters these opening lines, but it has concealed itself within an apparent banality. Moore's opening strategy is to muffle her own indictment of English prejudice in apparently inoffensive language, but her satire will eventually mount into a climactic parody of England's shallow judgments.

Having disposed of its titular subject—England—in three lines, the commenting voice of the poem, without a stanza break, proceeds to instance—still in travelogue form, but becoming more and more ignorant—aspects of other cultures of Europe and the Far East. Italy is disparagingly said to have "contrived" an overaesthetic epicureanism by "extracting" the "grossness" from its original recipes, timidly denaturing the typical offerings of its own indigenous cuisine. (Does this indictment for "grossness" bear examination?) Greece—the site, after all, of the Parthenon—displays visually to this voice, which is hostile to grand artifice, nothing but its alliterating rural "goats and gourds." These are quickly enough swept out of sight, but the philosophy of Greece is less easily ignored: the voice knows that Greece has recognized the vexing problem of illusions (Plato), but it has modified those illusions into a stunted realism (Aristotle) that so diminishes them in size that they fit into a single containing nest.

With France, a distrusted sophistication is said (in a conventional stereotype) to obscure practical function. One goes to a couturier in search of substance—a warm coat, perhaps—only to find that the cunning systems of French tailoring are more intriguing than the garment itself. The Paris couturier Erté has devised an evening gown so artfully cocooning the wearer (and here the poem quotes his hyperbolic French metaphor) that it becomes a chrysalis from which the buyer's body will emerge as a butterfly. Yes, the voice grants, fashion's inventions are "mysteries of construction," but the ingenuity of the craft diverts one from something surely more worthy: "substance at the core." Just as Moore does not bring the first four-line stanza to a close in England (suggesting that the country does not merit a whole stanza) but extends it into Italy's originally "gross" cuisine, so she does not close her second stanza within Europe, intimating that like England and Italy, Greece and France are rapidly shrinking in significance.

Instead the embodied voice runs on to the baffling culture of the East, reciting Western stereotypes of "the mysterious East" as superficial as those that England holds with respect to America. Some source must have informed Moore that "Chinese mystery snails" are so called because unlike snails from other countries, they give birth to live young. No less mysterious is the multistroke ideogram of classical Chinese, which Moore—allowing her own voice to intervene—excitedly names "emotional shorthand," remarkable for its visual compression of semantic meaning. (The word "shorthand" brings the poem into Moore's own modernity, revealing the contemporary writer's envy of such condensed, if inimitable, poetic means.) Conventional stereotypes return, as the East is said to offer repellent non-Western notions of what a precious jade artwork might represent—a cockroach—and its equally strange calm, its "imperturbability." (Moore imagines that her reader knows this stereotype of the Chinese character: the *Oxford English Dictionary* illustrates "imperturbability" with a quotation remarking on "the amazing stolidity and imperturbability of the Chinese in the face of all changes and disasters.") The voice becomes intellectually abstract

as it summarizes its preceding inventory of Asian art-
works: they are "all of museum quality," that is, removed
in time and therefore only partly intelligible to foreign
speculation on what fundamental aesthetic could prompt
an object such as the jade cockroach.

So FAR, the poem—after beginning with Moore's satire
on "baby rivers," has continued with a list of common ste-
reotypes for even the most ancient and revered cultures—
the Greek, the Chinese. But suddenly (and before we
quite realize it) the voice reverts to one Moore might have
heard during her visit to England: that of a critical English
observer being as dismissive of American phenomena as
she (and other Americans) have been of trivially noted
foreign peculiarities. As Moore "channels" the voice of
this supercilious critic, citing a throng of English stereo-
types of America's ignorant barbarity, she glances from
particular regions to the deplorable whole to offer indis-
putable evidence of British prejudice. Both the American
South and the American North, says the English aesthete,
display untended objects and objectionable customs: the
South exhibits a ramshackle version of a normally attrac-
tive English light carriage (named after Queen Victoria),
and the North discloses, shockingly, men actually smok-
ing cigars on the street. But those are only the beginning
of the expanding English list of American deficiencies
(petrifying into generalized stereotypes). Horror of hor-
rors, in America, with its error-spotted newspapers,
there are no proofreaders! Aware of the aristocratic silks
of the Far East, the "English" voice reproaches America
for having no silkworms, and—recalling the leisurely
prose of English essayists—the voice finds the curt prac-

tical discourse of America lacking in elegance. It has no digressions!

Other American defects are marked by implicit comparison with England: this is "a wild man's land" because it doesn't turn its prairies into beautiful English lawns; and still less is it conceivable that a culture should not have installed golf courses. America in 1920 is "links-less." And in synchrony with its uncultivated wildness of landscape, barren America is "language-less." Its inhabitants know no foreign tongues: its letters are written not in Spanish (even with the country's Mexican border), and certainly not in Greek or in Latin, because its population has not had the advantage of aristocratic English schooling. In fact, its letters do not rise even to the scribal vocabulary of shorthand, but—and here the English voice reaches its disbelieving climax—Americans write letters "in plain American that cats and dogs can read!" This is very funny, but in its reporting of English snobbery all too convincing in its taxonomic categorizing of subliterate Americans into "inferior" animal species—language-less cats and dogs. And not only do the English deem our written language elementary, they also reject our pronunciation as incorrect, denigrating the American flat "a" in "psalm" and "calm" in implicit praise of the open British "ah" which they (irrationally) find more suitable.

There ends Moore's sardonic parody of the way in which the English tourist isolates, misapprehends, and scorns various observed American features. Very well, says Moore, now not in the disguised voice of her subversive opening, nor in the imitative-of-stereotypes voice ranging through foreign territories, nor in the parodic voice of her British mockery, but in a didactic postcolonial voice we recognize as her own—very well, but upon such slender individual phenomena is it legitimate for the English to establish "continents of misapprehension"? She poses rapid questions of rebuttal: Why should a single difference of pronunciation justify the condemnation of a whole nation? Is there any logic to finding harmless mushrooms dangerous just because there exist "poisonous toadstools"? Is it reasonable to conclude that Americans possess a crass business appetite just because they are mettlesome, or to argue that they are hasty (say, in drawing conclusions) just because they are heated (say, in argument)?

There the questions break off. Moore knows how embarrassing it is, if you have been proud of your own precision, to discover that you have misapprehended something; it shames you to realize that you have not studied the object of your curiosity with sufficient attention. In contrast with the entertaining sequence of her travelogue-of-stereotypes, her parody of the British tourist-in-America, and her rapid questions, Moore couches in a single dry and damning sentence her own redeeming confession of past prejudice:

> To have misapprehended the matter, is to
> have confessed
> that one has not looked far enough.

Indicting general prejudice (found worldwide and not least in herself) and admitting general fallibility, the poet asks by implication whether we Americans have tried to see an England larger than the one displaying only unimpressive rivers and thin threads of liturgical sound. Have the English tried to see us beyond our different pronunciation, our absence of enthusiasm for golf, our frequency of typographical errors, and our lack of acquaintance with foreign languages?

Another list follows, the very opposite of the initial intemperate list of superficial remarks from English observers and the ignorant stereotypes we ourselves might use in describing foreign countries in Europe or Asia. Moore's last list is a heterogeneous one, offering examples of what she calls "noted superiority." These—based on her own study and the learning of scholars—range from the wisdom of China (a contrast to citing its jade cockroaches) to the "discernment" of Egypt (harbinger of Western literacy), to the unsurpassed torrent of emotion in Hebrew verbs (more valuable than shorthand), to the nonchalance of *The Compleat Angler* (in Moore's excerpt from Walton beginning "I envy nobody"). Such "noted superiority," Moore claims, bears flowers which will generate the eventual fruit of a country's cultural cornucopia. Addressing those who dismiss her cherished America, Moore asks a single logical question: if one hasn't yet "stumbled upon" examples of such superiority in America, does it follow that it does not exist here? (The absurdity of generalizing from absence of evidence to evidence of absence is self-evident.) She appends an uninsistent truth: that such "noted superiority" "has never been confined to one locality." This irrefutable rebuke—superbly understated—disposes not only of the contemptuous English observer who prompted the poem, but also of Americans invoking petrified stereotypes of other cultures.

IF, HAVING followed Moore's argument and filled in all that is implied within it, we ask what kind of a poem "England" is, from what notion of poetry it must issue, we see that for Moore poetry must be heterogeneous to be interesting: it must admit learning, argument, allusion, inference, and conclusions, but it also must permit fantasy, comedy, satire, mockery, and uncircumscribed linguistic possibility. Jokes about literate cats and dogs are allowed to occupy the same art-space as Chinese snails and Chinese wisdom. *The Compleat Angler*'s unworldly admiration for a fellow-fisherman can coexist with scholarly admiration of the "torrent of emotion" in the verbs of a non-English, non-European, non-Chinese language— Hebrew; the intellectual wit of calling individual ideograms "emotional shorthand" may be harbored next to a down-to-earth example of the trivial sonic phenomenon of the flat American "a" in "psalm." Moore's readers— warned by her deceptive touristic subterfuge that what seems a tender picture of rural England can evolve into a freewheeling farce on English snobbery, and develop in turn into an indictment of all human prejudice—discover at the same moment, on another plane, that a succession of equal four-line stanzas—even if they do not scan, even if they do not rhyme—can formally identify the object on the page as a poem. Unlike the primary aim of prose, which is logical exposition, the object of verse—defined as such by its formal patterning—is chiefly a display of the imagination delighting in its own activity.

In any writer, the drive to create dazzling play in the chosen medium is often accompanied, often somewhat later in the process of creation, by an equal need to fill a lack in the surrounding historical, ethical, or cognitive context. What, in the artist's view, does the contemporary world need to hear or to see? Along with aesthetic joy, a poem must offer, said Horace, something of use to the reader. At their best, Moore's crisp intuitions of fallible human nature, as they discover a moving analogy from her zoo of undomesticated animals, arrive at precisely such a seamless junction of wisdom and delight. Just as Moore was drawn to translate the fables of La Fontaine in which a beast-fable is followed by a moral, so she could rarely resist, within her exhibits of rarity or oddity, a kernel of philosophical epigram: "It has never been confined to one locality"; "we prove, we do not explain our birth."

Unmarried—and jesting, in her long poem "Marriage," that marriage takes "all one's criminal ingenuity / to avoid"—Moore was, after her mother died, for the first time alone. Missing her mother and her deceased contemporaries, Moore made friends with the larger American world, writing poems about sports figures, including Muhammad Ali, jockeys, and baseball players. She wore, when she left her Brooklyn apartment for the city, an eccentric ensemble of a black tricorn hat and black cape. (Her first cape, in youth, was sewn by her mother, and wearing one as her distinguishing garment must have kept her mother's presence nearby.) She became something of a public pet, genially throwing out the first pitch to open the baseball season. In those later years, the conspicuous old woman photographed by the newspapers seems far from the young poet praised by Eliot or the dauntless editor of *The Dial*, which gave her, with its office, a five-year daily base among New York writers. Wallace Stevens and William Carlos Williams found her an enchanting companion. "All great men," said Yeats, "are owls, scarecrows, by the time their fame has come." That may be true of great women, too.

Moore created a powerful and influential style, an inimitable one—although Auden and others imitated her use of syllables, instead of accents, to determine line-lengths; and Elizabeth Bishop, James Merrill, and Amy Clampitt were indebted to her rendition of the visual world and her unpredictable montages and collages of surface terrain. Later poets have both softened and sweetened her bristly or spiny poetic, smoothed her ungainly ostrich-gait. It still takes work to internalize a Moore poem—to look up its unfamiliar allusions to Erté or Chinese snails, to comb through its intricate syntax, to deduce which philosophical or psychological problem has generated its tight-knit emblem-illustrations. But after gaining a footing in Moore's irregular territory, one can arrive at a relish for the very oddities that originally seemed obstacles. The maze once entered and its center attained, one luxuriates in the sound-world of an apparently effortless chamber music.

And precisely because most protest-poems are by their content alone made unrelievedly earnest, a reader can be charmed by a poet's decision to choose the weapon of wit. The American Moore was not the only writer to feel the lash of British dismissal: the Irish, the Australian, the Welsh, the Caribbean writer felt it, too. The best parody of the maliciously patronizing English manner is D. H. Lawrence's corrosive poem on English hypocrisy, "The English Are So Nice!" (Lawrence was English, and his father was a miner: he was well acquainted with English condescension.) I quote his poem here only as an example of a protest-poem which, although resembling Moore's in intensity and comic bitterness, abandons the allusive for the apparently artless. After its deceptive opening lines with their third-person description of the English as "awfully nice," Lawrence's poem quickly devolves into a rendition of the truly awful sentiments of prejudice as they appear in bourgeois conversation. What that "niceness" conveys, its scorpion-sting—as experienced by the hapless human object of its aggression—appears as early as the sixth line and stings its object fatally in its lethal xenophobic conclusion:

> The English are so nice
> so awfully nice
> they're the nicest people in the world.

> And what's more, they're very nice about being nice
> about your being nice as well!
> If you're not nice, they soon make you feel it.

> Americans and French and Germans and so on
> they're all very well
> but they're not *really* nice, you know.
> They're not nice in *our* sense of the word, are they
>   now?

> That's why one doesn't have to take them seriously.
> We must be nice to them, of course,
> of course, naturally—
> But it doesn't really matter what you say to them,
> they don't really understand—
> you can just say anything to them:
> be nice, you know, just nice
> but you must never take them seriously, they
>   wouldn't understand,
> just be nice, you know! Oh, fairly nice,
> not too nice of course, they take advantage—
> but nice enough, just nice enough
> to let them feel they're not quite as nice as they
>   might be.

The social convention of covering all possible situations with the "unobjectionable" word *nice* wears so thin, even to the ears of its English utterer, that the poem eventually slips into the openly prejudiced "not *really* nice," the disdainful "they wouldn't understand," and finally into the spiteful and fearful "they take advantage."

Lawrence, the master of eloquence, exposes by apparently artless mimicry the appalling verbal poverty of the English middle class as they scorn and fear all foreigners, even English-speaking ones. Masquerading as one of the insular English, he betters them at their own game, while Moore, exhibiting foreign stereotypes of other cultures, shames American provinciality as well as English snobbery. Both poets, with their wit, hit their mark.

Any young woman scholar of my era encountered prejudiced male teachers and colleagues, but along with the prejudiced I encountered the kind and the just. Lyric poets writing protest-poems risk simplifying the world into a melodrama of the good and the evil, thereby rendering their representations unreal. (It is of course an equally coarse assertion that there were "very fine people on both sides.") Pure parody such as Lawrence's "The English Are So Nice!" is by its very genre not obligated to justice of representation: justice is immediately perceived as the opposite of the parodic. But lyric poets of protest are obliged to incriminate themselves if their remarks about others' faults are to be believed. Moore redeems "England," in the end, by including in it a genuine—if impersonally put—confession of her own past stereotyping of the foreign. Unlike the believable poets, the prejudiced ones never include themselves among the sinners.

How to Talk to God

Holy Sonnet 14

Batter my heart, three-person'd God; for, you
As yet but knocke, breathe, shine, and seeke to mend;
That I may rise, and stand, o'erthrow mee,'and bend
Your force, to breake, blowe, burn and make me new.
I, like an usurpt towne, to'another due,
Labour to'admit you, but Oh, to no end,
Reason your viceroy in mee, mee should defend,
But is captiv'd, and proves weake or untrue,
Yet dearely'I love you,'and would be lov'd faine,
But am betroth'd unto your enemie,
Divorce mee,'untie, or breake that knot againe,
Take mee to you, imprison mee, for I
Except you'enthrall mee, never shall be free,
Nor ever chast, except you ravish mee.

JOHN DONNE

⌐

C AN "OLD" POEMS, written in a vanished culture, be rescued for a contemporary reader, or will their brilliance be lost? I will fasten my hope here on John Donne's spectacular fourteenth sonnet of his *Holy Sonnets*, published posthumously in 1633. But what are we rescuing in such a case? A statement? A fragment of autobiography? A portrait? Yeats, the finest poet of the twentieth century, offers an answer that seems to me the true one: a lyric poem is a simulacrum of a succession of human moods, conducting us through their rapid transitions and self-contradictions. The melody of the poem enters the reader invisibly, as if it were a transfusion. Yeats, an intense absorber of English poetry from the fourteenth century to the twentieth, had to ask himself, for his own instruction, what it was about certain past poems that made them endure. Since the passage of time tends to make prose—essays, sermons, philosophies, manifestos—decay, why should we prize past poems at all? Is a poem published in 1633 as outmoded for us as the theology or the science of its era?

Yeats argues that only one trait of human life is universal and recurrent in all human beings: the experiencing of moods over a lifetime. Our general terms for emotions are boring: "I'm depressed," "I was so glad." Experiencing a mood, however, is not boring at all: it is enlivening; it tells us that we are alive. (Robert Lowell observed in a lecture that "a poem is an event, not the record of an event.") Yeats dismisses both intellectual culture and natural phenomena as fundamental sources for poetry, claiming instead that only the moods are eternal, always formidably present everywhere and in all times, and recognized by each generation of human beings. The moods are "fire-born," generated not from the material levels of earth, water, and air, but from a deathless fire, the invisible energy that sustains life. The moods are neither calm nor obedient: to the soul they are a "rout," an ever-present and uncontrollable throng of disturbing visitors. Here is Yeats's tiny two-beat poem on that overpowering and rebellious and memorable throng:

The Moods

Time drops in decay,
Like a candle burnt out,

> And the mountains and woods
> Have their day, have their day;
> What one in the rout
> Of the fire-born moods
> Has fallen away?

Answer: not one. Not a single mood, Yeats believes, has ever been lost from the repertory of personal consciousness, whether registered in human beings or reflected in poems. Contemporary readers recognize without effort every mood in Shakespeare's sonnets: moods of infatuation, love, disgust, dismay, anger, wonder, meditation; moods sublime and shameful, trivial and tragic, coursing surprisingly in and through our own veins. In "Poem," Elizabeth Bishop wrote, on seeing an old painting, "Heavens, I recognize the place, I know it!" She had been there before.

To Yeats, a lyric poem exists because of the poet's felt compulsion to trace the contour of the complex, invisible, shifting, alarming, and passionate moods constantly pressing on human beings from infancy on, and continuing (unceasing in variety and unpredictable in evolution) until death. The fierce obligation to animate the human moods on paper through a template of sonic form is an urgent one to poets, but they find the task an almost impossible one, since moods are so distinctly shaded in idiosyncratic fashion. My mood of melancholy may bear a "family resemblance" to yours, but it will manifest itself, linguistically speaking, in a different pacing, an unfamiliar scene, a new minor key, legato in lieu of staccato, syncopated rather than regular—and if its conceptual and melodic expression in language does not become an experience for the reader, the poem has failed as the unique internal energy-transfer it must aim to become.

To rescue a lyric poem of the Western past is to feel how deeply we have already encountered its human moods, although this may be the first time we have seen them illustrated in just this shading, at just this pace, with just this degree of unnerving precision. Poets exhibit a set of moods indescribable by any generality. In a poem we watch a blurred interior contour take on a distinct face, which turns out to be our own: "Heavens, I recognize the place!" At that point we can voice the words as if they have been born in us. The poets may be making distinctions that we have never made, but as soon as the words create a dynamic life in us, we are struck by their accuracy. Shakespeare, for instance, will offer a taunting definition of a certain inscrutable form of behavior, and complex though it is, we shiver and recognize the species of persons who toy with the emotions of others while themselves remaining, in a chilling sense, impeccable. Such a definition, in its obliqueness, is far from one we could have composed ourselves, but as we read Sonnet 94, we miserably recognize Shakespeare's portrait of such seducers—

> They that have pow'r to hurt, and will do none,
> That do not do the thing they most do show,
> Who, moving others, are themselves as stone,
> Unmovèd, cold, and to temptation slow . . .

The pain in the lines transmits a lover's struggle to express—but in an abstract and impersonal form—his shameful infatuation with a narcissistic deceiver. The sonnet's oblique concealment of the intrinsic nature and actions of such a person requires us to struggle, like the lover, to ascertain the truth. Recognition of our parallel struggle awakens the poem in us.

DONNE'S HOLY Sonnet 14, like Shakespeare's Sonnet 94, creates within us the experience of a disturbed sufferer. And it therefore provokes puzzled questions: why, instead of simply addressing God as a single deity, do I (as Donne's speaker, henceforth referred to as "D" to distinguish him from Donne the author) feel called upon by my predicament to address all three "Persons" of the Christian Trinity, Father, Son, and Holy Spirit, only to revert to a single God after I no longer "need" the Trinity? A modern reader may be unlikely to recall the two contested Christian concepts acted out within the poem: is a human being a creature predestined by a Calvinist God to eternal damnation or salvation, or is he its more humane opposite, a person endowed by the Creator with free will? Modernity has naturalized "predestination" as ordinary causality (historical, biological, psychoanalytic), and as the theology of creation drops out of the modern debate, the reality of "free will" becomes uncertain. Yet the ancient opposition of determinism and free will persists equally in the modern mind: Can I free myself from addiction by sheer will? If not, is there any other recourse? D, finding himself inextricably addicted to promiscuity, seeks external aid to cure him. Today D might look for psychological or medical help, but in seventeenth-century England he calls on God.

As past eras drop away, not only do past concepts (the Trinity, predestination) become extinct, but also, for non-Latinists, there occurs the effacement of etymological meaning. The original English readers of Donne's circulating manuscripts were highly educated Christians for whom Latin was almost as familiar as English. Such readers would have known that the Latin noun *spiritus* (as in "the Holy Spirit") is, in English translation, "the breath," which, when converted to a verb ("to breathe") and intensified—as D demands—becomes the poem's "blowe." Similarly, the Christian reader would have seen the pun by which the Son of God is said to be the Sun. Donne the theologian (see his extravagant later sermons) has perhaps experienced, and certainly analyzed, the complicated and conflicting emotions surging through the speaker of Holy Sonnet 14: the speaker knows the redemptive promise of a virtuous life, but is aware as well of the troubling guilt of persistent wrongdoing, the unrelenting fear of continued sexual addiction, and the defensive excuses usually offered by the addicted.

Yet almost all commentators have believed (as we can see from the exhausting number of their remarks quoted in the *Donne Variorum*) that Donne's speaker is "praying" to God. That description seems dubious to me. Do we know what Donne would consider a prayer acceptable to God? Yes, we do: in Holy Sonnet 7, a repentant sinner, recalling Saint Paul's consoling words, "where sin abounded, grace did much more abound" (Romans 5:20), can feel hope for his own salvation. Imagining the dead on Judgment Day, stationed "there" in the afterlife (when it has become too late to repent), the sinner prays as a penitent, "here" on "lowly ground," that he will be taught by God how to repent in time:

> But let them [the dead] sleepe, Lord, and mee
>   mourne a space,
> For, if above all these, my sinnes abound,
> 'Tis late to aske abundance of thy grace,
> When wee are there; here on this lowly ground,
> Teach mee how to repent; for that's as good
> As if thou'hadst seal'd my pardon, with thy blood.

This speaker's humble "Teach mee how to repent" sounds nothing like D's insistent imperatives hurled at God's ear. Donne-the-composing-author would of course have recognized the difference between the penitent speaker's acceptable "prayer" (an acknowledgment of sin, with a plea to be instructed in virtue by God) and D's persistent (and improper) reproaches blaming God for His insufficient effectiveness. Still addicted, still unrepentant, D rails at his putative savior.

Readers with a hazy sense that any speech addressing God can be called a "prayer" have not understood that no acceptable prayer can reproach God (who is perfect) or can suggest (to a divinity who is eternal) that he alter his actions in time. Rather, a believer's prayers address a God who is ever benevolent and ever the same. But "As yet"—says D (intemperately calling for an improved future from his silent God) "you / As yet but knocke." Christopher Hitchens sardonically remarked in *Mortality* that the person who prays "is the one who thinks that god has arranged matters all wrong, but who also thinks that he can instruct god how to put them right." That epigram exactly sums up what is expressed in the first twelve lines of Donne's sonnet, while in the last two lines D will discover—in the cleverest way—an acceptable alternative to propose: D will retain the helplessness he has maintained throughout, and God will bring him to salvation without external force.

MOST READERS have assumed that it is the "real Donne" —the historical authorial one—who speaks Holy Sonnet 14; he certainly speaks *in propria persona* within other sonnets. The commentators quoted in the *Donne Variorum* consistently mistake D's actual speech-acts by employing in their paraphrases—besides the actual word "pray"—a number of synonyms: "Donne" *entreats, beseeches, implores, pleads,* and so on. But the speaker of the poem does *not* perform these religiously acceptable acts: rather, he demands, he reproaches, he insists, he complains, and he consistently represents himself as a victim of God's inadequate assistance. And is it credible that the authorial Donne is here speaking as "himself," when the impertinent D apparently does not understand the legitimate ways to address God and the reverent posture suitable for acceptable prayer? (Even the pious person about to pronounce a prayer has to beg God to find it acceptable.) It is the visible disharmony between the Donne who writes the other *Holy Sonnets* and the protesting "D" who speaks "Batter my heart" that compels a necessary distinction between author and speaker. This is always an awkward procedure because our instinct is to merge the author and the "I" of the poem, but it becomes necessary to separate them whenever there is a discrepancy (as when Donne speaks as a woman in "Breake of Day").

The historical Donne, author and courtier, was raised during the Reformation in an intensely Roman Catholic family, but later took orders in the English Church and eventually became Dean of St. Paul's in London. Expert from youth in the diction of faith, he would not have seriously entertained D's notion that he can harangue God on how to better His actions, nor would he have characterized D's successive ultimatums as "prayers." D's expostulations to God arrive as a torrent of imperatives beginning with explosive *b*'s: *batter, bend, breake, blowe, burn,* and again *breake.* These are not words of entreaty but words of offended entitlement. In one of Donne's strokes of authorial wit, he exposes the self-serving reason for D's triple mustering (in his battle against Satan) of all three Persons of the Trinity, Father, Son, and Holy Spirit. Resentfully, D has been reflecting, "There are three of Them: why are They not more efficacious in battling the enemy? Surely the divine Persons have more available power than Satan!" But the Trinity disappears from the poem when D recognizes how improbable it is that he, the sinner, will receive supernatural reinforcements: he reimagines the military battle as a single combat with Satan; and once he drops the Trinitarian summons, D always addresses God in the singular (revealing that it was a matter of temporary military expediency to summon the three Persons in his first lines).

In his mood of rebellion, D demands more successful actions by all three Persons. Yes, God the Father created him, but His creature (now addicted to disobedience and sinful sexual expression) has come to grief. God *must* (commands D) create a replacement for D's "old" self and make a whole "new" human being; it would be a mistake on God's part merely to *mend* the old one. Since God the Son is (punningly) the Sun, he has the power to *burn*, to consume the "old" self utterly, making room for the "new" one; certainly he can do better than merely *shine*. God the Holy Spirit has so far merely deigned to *breathe*; instead he should *blowe,* as he did in the guise of a "rushing mighty wind" when the apostles came together after Christ's ascension into heaven: "And when the day of Pentecost was fully come, [the apostles] were all with one accord in one place. And suddenly there came a sound from heaven as of a rushing mighty wind, and it filled all the house where they were sitting" (Acts 2:1–2).

But in spite of D's rising decibels, each person of the Trinity has continued mildly in known ways. God the

Father merely *mends* the damaged being; God the Son will do no more than *knocke* at the door of the heart, not *batter* it or *burn* it with fire; and God the Holy Spirit gently *breathes*, will not *blowe* the heart's door open. In Donne's emphatic arrangement of D's excited verbs, the desired act always pushes itself into place before the current one:

> *batter* ⟵——————— *knocke*
> *blowe* ⟵——————— *breathe*
> *burn* ⟵———————*shine*
> *make new* ⟵——————— *seek to mend*
> *breake* ⟵——————— *seek to mend*
> *bend your force* ⟵——————— *knocke*
> *breake* ⟵——————— *seek to mend*

God's gentle present actions in the second column are "feminized" by their "weakness" vis-à-vis the powerful and explosive masculinity of all the "*b*" words in the first column. In an impatient argument, D urges his "masculine" verbs on the Trinity as a set of actions preferable to those "weak" ones that God has so far been resorting to. "Batter" the speaker's heart—with what? A "battering ram," the weapon that can conquer a city at the end of a siege. D irritably repudiates the feeble single "knocke" in favor of troop action. (He has thereby explained his invoking of all three Persons of the Trinity, since a battering ram must be wielded by more than one attacker.) The satisfying resonance of the repeated "*b*'s" exposes the speaker's exultation at having piled up (in prospect) so many reinforcements of his army. As D blames God for his own helpless continuation in a sinful state, he does not shame himself by naming his sins, but rather implies that

God could nullify any and all sins if He would exert some energetic force.

Abandoning the hope of a Trinity-staffed battle, after the silent absence of the summoned Persons, D has decided on single combat—a duel with Satan. He imagines himself, in a plaintive simile, not as an actor in battle, but as the victim of an unnamed usurper of the throne of his own terrain: "I, like an usurpt towne." His mood becomes one of self-excuse, as he releases a vague explanatory flashback (but one lacking many crucial details): "Once I was a well-governed city, ruled by God's viceroy, Reason. Then a wicked usurper assumed [but how?] the throne of the viceroy." The blurred narrative of victimization continues: Reason, the absent viceroy, is now a captive (but whose, and why?). "The usurpation must have happened" (says D, blaming the viceroy) either because Reason was weak and is now imprisoned or—a far worse concluding speculation—God's viceroy has turned traitor, has been "untrue," and is now a minion of Satan. D claims that his own strong efforts to admit God to the "usurpt" city have been frustrated by Reason's traitorous secession. Would the authorial Donne think to deceive God by such a tale? Of course not. It is the speaker who resorts to self-excuse, revealing himself as a hypocrite, once again blaming others (if not God, then Satan) for his plight.

As D continues his narrative into the immediate present, Donne-the-author turns the sonnet in a different direction, changing his rhyme scheme to alert his reader. The first eight lines (rhyming *abbaabba*) had created, in "embraced rhymes," the octave of an "Italian" sonnet, but the closing six lines adopt a "Shakespearean" sestet, an alternately rhymed quatrain plus a couplet (*cdcdee*). Such a hybrid form announces a fundamental change in mood from octave to sestet, but we are not yet aware what it may be, although we feel the mood change as the speaker voices a single dejected admission: "Yet dearely' I love you." Still sinning, D quickly takes on a false pathos, asserting in self-defense that although he loves God dearly, and is eager to be loved in return, yet he has waked to find himself dismayingly "betrothed" to God's enemy, Satan. How can that have happened, apparently without his conscious knowledge? D has voluntarily (if bafflingly) "tied the knot"—as the colloquial phrase has it—in a solemn public promise to marry. By some sorcery, D tells God, he has been betrayed into a contract with a seductive unnamed "enemie." As usual, D never imputes any agency or blame to himself for his condition: the betrothal has merely "happened" (Donne discloses D's attitude by the passive voice of "am betroth'd," rather than "I betrothed myself").

Donne-the-author must now reveal that D, even after admitting the fact of the sinful betrothal, believes that he cannot extract himself from it, and has not changed his expectation that it is God's responsibility to free him. Donne points out this truth by D's voluntary return to the violence of his initial address to God (with the telling repetition of his earlier injunction, "breake," implying that he is still reproaching God's inertia). "Divorce me," he cries, from the promised marriage (appealing to the Jewish law permitting such action); "untie" or "breake" that quasi-marital Gordian knot of betrothal. The pitch of the voice rises ever higher as the sinner's mood worsens. In protest against his apparent helplessness. D bursts out (the vowel echoing the doubly resounding "breake"), "Take mee to you, imprison mee." In this histrionic climax, D unwittingly parallels the action he says he desires ("imprison mee") with Satan's action as he (supposedly) imprisoned God's defeated and "captiv'd" viceroy. When a speaker—even unconsciously—wants God to reproduce an action by Satan, that speaker is emphatically not the authorial Donne but rather an imagined (and faulty) sexual sinner.

Although the poem has been composed of a string of verbs of demand, God has responded to none of them (not even to the "milder" suggestion of "untie") and D's despair has not yet been alleviated by any merciful act. Casting hither and yon for a verb which will move God to save him, D has so far run through a thesaurus of imperatives, always maintaining his own innocence, always making others responsible for his sin or professing ignorance of its cause. Does D sound here like a man praying? "A broken and a contrite heart, O God, thou wilt not despise," says the Psalmist. Has D, up to this point, manifested a mood either heartbroken or contrite? To the contrary, he has remained wronged and accusatory. He has, in short, not been "praying" (or "entreating" or "imploring" or "beseeching" or "pleading") at all; he has been rebuking God as too mild in his solicitations of the heart, too weak to prevent the usurpation of the heart-town by Satan, and even too timid to untie the betrothal-knot.

Though remaining wholly passive, D—after the bitter mood in which he scourges God's inertia—is enabled to discover verbs which *will* change his state, *will* embody the necessary conditions for his restoration to virtue. As before, he expects God to be the active agent of his salvation. However, in the most linguistically "magical" move of the poem, D is rescued by the ability of his former language to mutate. Donne-the-author succeeds in letting D keep his desired passivity as he investigates the possibilities of salvation through etymology and grammar. Language saves D by presenting inspiring new verbs to him, translations into metaphor of his earlier literal claims. "Imprison me!" he has cried, and language (through its authorial tutor, Donne) whispers to him, "You know, there *are* other versions of the words you are thinking of using: for 'imprison' you could more aptly say *'enthrall,'* since a 'thrall' is a prisoner, and 'enthralled' means '(voluntarily) imprisoned by enchantment.'" The Muse of Language offers an additional counsel: "And for the forcible 'rape' (which must have preceded your unwilled 'betrothal' to Satan) you could more properly ask God to 'ravish' you; the word indeed issues from the same root as 'rape'—*rapere*—but like 'rapt' and 'rapture' is metaphorical." At this moment, transmitting the revelations of the Muse of Language, Donne the poet feels, twice, the joy of the *mot juste:*

> for I
> Except you'enthrall mee, never shall be free,
> Nor ever chast, except you ravish mee.

The words "free" and "chast[e]" cast a light backwards, summing up the whole preceding narrative. By naming the virtues he desires—to be "free" and "chast[e]"—D confesses his hitherto unnamed sins, which are an enslavement to wrongdoing and sexual promiscuity.

BUT HOW was the magical revelation of the "right language" induced in D the sinner? It was, I think, by the

one truth in D's outburst at the turning-point indicated
by the changing of the rhyme-scheme: at that moment
D recalls a deep past attachment to God, one still pres-
ent in memory, which he longs to rediscover. The subdu-
ing of mood and the drop of voice in his admission "Yet
dearely'I love you,'and would be lov'd faine" measure D's
subsequent despair when he feels himself unloved and in
danger of damnation. That he has remembered, amid his
frantic demands, his past happiness when he felt loved by
God suggests that in his exhaustion he is taking stock of
the better past as well as the wretched present.

In his blasting cascade of imperatives, D has been driven
into a corner where his vocabulary of wrath is exhausted.
Recalling his last mood of happiness, turning his face at
last to the God he has been excoriating, remembering the
past state in which he loved and was loved before sex and
rebellion possessed him, and implicitly confessing his sins
and his desire to be free and chaste, he hopes to regain
equilibrium in a final "steady state": "I can be free only
when you enthrall me; I can be chaste only when you
ravish me." With "ravish" Donne is invoking the meta-
phorical sense of *rapere*—to abduct, to carry away—as
he does in the Holy Sonnet on his wife's death. Quoting
St. Paul's recollection of "a man" (probably himself) who
was "caught up to the third heaven" (2 Corinthians 12:2),
Donne remarks in Holy Sonnet 17 of his young wife that
her soul was "early into heaven ravished."

In the mind of D, as he remembers his happier state,
God's goodness and beauty replace the rival claims of a
putatively adult independence and putatively passionate
sexual experience. Donne-the-author arranges the final
"Shakespearean" couplet in the figure called chiasmus, or
"crossing." In this figure of speech (which always implies

a speaker's intellectual control of his earlier affliction), the etymologically metaphorical verbs become the "outside" brackets, while the "inside" brackets are the adjectives of longed-for virtue—enthrall:free::chaste:ravish. Chiasmus is always a figure of forethought, showing the conscious close of emotional distress. Using "linear" terms of the conditions of his salvation, D would say, "Unless you enthrall and ravish me, I will never be free and chaste." Chiasmus, using "bracketing" terms, "locks" the "solution" into the completeness of coming full circle, ratified by the happy discovery of the two metaphorical verbs permitting D to solve his despair while allowing him to regain—without carrying out any activities to save himself—the feeling of being loved by God.

I can imagine that Donne's whole poem was generated by his delighted discovery of the particular properties and the grammatical parallels of the verbs "enthrall" and "ravish." Both verbs require a direct object, and as Donne constructs a scene in which "God" is the agent of these verbs, while D is the direct object, the poet obtains the psychological continuation of his speaker's desire for passivity. If D were to speak here in the first person, he would have to render the facts in the *passive* voice: "I am enthralled by you": "I am ravished by you." Rather, the Son's radiant presence (as the "Sun") is indeed the agent, but not by an act of exerted force: rather, the divine light diffuses itself eternally without needing to effect any isolated action in time. When D laments "Yet I love you" in his bafflement, he has not yet realized that God requires nothing of him except to bask in the "Sun's" shining warmth (erasing his angry wish that God should "burn" him). War—the first metaphorical axis of D's sinful state—miraculously, in the warmth of God's uninterrupted "shining," recedes from memory; and Love—the second axis—mutates from erotic addiction to *agape* or Christian love, charity.

Granted, to understand "Batter my heart" in this century, the modern reader has to search out some aspects of Christianity in an encyclopedia and check the etymologies of two crucial verbs in a dictionary. But the reader is repaid by being thrust through an electric sequence of tumultuous moods, enacting them in person and experiencing them as virtual events. No other poem will transfuse agitation into the reader in exactly these dimensions, this angry and disturbed and excited doubt of one's own will as a reliable agent of virtue, followed by the vivid sensation that God will not refuse salvation, but will, by a steady infusion of light, transform spiritual passivity into a cherished mutuality of enthralled self and ravished soul. The linguistic journey through moods so violently conducted and so exquisitely rewarded makes the reader see the speaker of the poem as a recognizable mirror of human anxiety and human sensibility. Anxiety and sensibility, never absent from the psyche, will arouse in readers, in the moment of immense final relief of the poem, a voice almost four hundred years old, making a faithful traversal of their own personal troubled and chaotic—but universal and timeless—moods of shame, perplexity, anger, resentment, and love.

The New Statue

Morning Song

Love set you going like a fat gold watch.
The midwife slapped your footsoles, and your bald cry
Took its place among the elements.

Our voices echo, magnifying your arrival. New statue.
In a drafty museum, your nakedness
Shadows our safety. We stand round blankly as walls.

I'm no more your mother
Than the cloud that distills a mirror to reflect its own slow
Effacement at the wind's hand.

All night your moth-breath
Flickers among the flat pink roses. I wake to listen:
A far sea moves in my ear.

One cry, and I stumble from bed, cow-heavy and floral
In my Victorian nightgown.
Your mouth opens clean as a cat's. The window square

Whitens and swallows its dull stars. And now you try
Your handful of notes;
The clear vowels rise like balloons.

19 February 1961
SYLVIA PLATH

WHEN MY son was born, I was shocked to realize that among all the poems I knew, hardly any were about a baby or about becoming a mother. For a long time I had been accustomed to find, on almost any occasion of substance, a line of verse rising unbidden to consciousness, unerringly telling me what I was feeling. But the joyous line that had risen spontaneously and immediately at childbirth—"For unto us a child is born, unto us a son is given"—was followed by no others, and an unaccustomed silence lay heavy on my mind with the absence of any resonance between my life and a poem commenting on it.

One of the poems that I did know (remembered from childhood because my mother had quoted it) opened with a putative dialogue between a mother and her newborn baby:

> Where did you come from, baby dear?
> Out of the everywhere into here.

I eventually read the poem (by George MacDonald, the Victorian novelist), and while I recognized the wit in the graphic decline of the enormous invisible "every*where*" into the diminished visible "*here*," as a whole the fantasy was too sentimental for me:

> Feet, whence did you come, you darling things?
> From the same box as the cherubs' wings.

I flinched at that as I did at Mother's Day cards.

When, as an adult, I read Blake's *Songs of Experience*, I at last found (in "Infant Sorrow") a newborn baby speaking credibly of its own birth-agony. Outraged by its forced eruption from warm amniotic comfort into an unfamiliar and chilling world, and rebelling against both its restrictive swaddling clothes and its father's constraining arms, the helpless baby screams cries unintelligible to the horrified parents, who wonder what demonic force is obscured behind the cloud of their struggling infant's flesh. The exhausted baby, in its first intellectual moment, thinks it best to retreat into a silent sulk:

> My mother groand! my father wept.
> Into the dangerous world I leapt:
> Helpless, naked, piping loud;
> Like a fiend hid in a cloud.
>
> Struggling in my fathers hands:
> Striving against my swadling bands:
> Bound and weary I thought best
> To sulk upon my mothers breast.

The poet—imagining the words a terrified newborn might shriek if it had language—exposes the pieties of the usual "baby poem." A fierce empathy with the baby's sufferings at birth prompted Blake's glimpse here into the disillusioned state he called "Experience," while his earlier "Infant Joy" (from *Songs of Innocence*) screened out the real baby, entering instead into the new mother's projection (onto her actually silent baby) of her own self-absorbed joy. The mother's fantasy that her infant (the Latin *infans* means "unable to speak") begins life by complaining of its lack of a name prompts, with exquisite reciprocity, her own mirroring response: "What shall I call thee?" The baby declares that its name is "Joy," and the mother, completing the circuit of dialogue, utters a blessing: "Sweet joy befall thee!" As the dialogue opens, the baby speaks first:

> I have no name
> I am but two days old.—
> What shall I call thee?
> I happy am
> Joy is my name,—
> Sweet joy befall thee!

The whole second stanza belongs to the mother, as she ecstatically reinforces (with "Pretty" and "Sweet") the exclusive symbiotic delight of shared harmonic naming-and-echoing. The baby smiles while the joyful mother sings, and her repetition of the sixth line is no longer a wish but a concurrent fact, confirmed by the song, the smile, and the closing period:

> Pretty joy!
> Sweet joy but two days old.
> Sweet joy I call thee:
> Thou dost smile.
> I sing the while
> Sweet joy befall thee.

The ecstatic narcissism of this (imagined) dialogue is surreally critiqued by Blake in "Infant Sorrow." The "experienced" mother—disabused of her naïve girlish image of a loving dialogue with her child—is groaning in her birth-pains, the father is weeping in alarm, and the baby is furious.

These were to me real poems, confronting both the "innocent" virginal fantasy of purely joyful motherhood and the dark trauma of experience—both equally human, both requiring acknowledgment, both known to any sheltered girl who has become a mother.

AND SO, when I first saw Sylvia Plath's "Morning Song," her narrative of how a clueless young wife gradually becomes able to love her infant, I felt astonished relief. A modern poet had at last told the story of her gradual initiation into motherhood. As "Morning Song" opens, a couple stand awkwardly around their newborn baby, conceived in love but now an unfamiliar stranger to its parents. Petrified by anxiety into immobile "statues," the couple fear what they may have done in admitting a "New statue" into their uneasy "museum." The house is now merely the curator of its own past, a museum of former selves, unable to conceive of a future with this unfathomable inhabitant. The naked creature intrudes into the scene by making an unfamiliar animal sound, while the parents, in joint unease, echo and magnify, with their adult voices, the infant's inarticulate cry.

Plath's wonderfully unexpected third stanza expresses, in its peculiarly slow and evolving syntax, the mother's gradual perception-by-negatives of her new state: "I'm no more your mother / Than. . . ." The husband and the collective "We" vanish permanently from the scene, leaving the wife, a single "I," to clarify her relation to the child she addresses. Unable as yet to conceive of that relation in human terms, she resorts instead, in the pivot of the poem, to the vague climatic terms of cloud and wind. She progresses haltingly to acknowledge that in giving birth she has signed the warrant for her own eventual death, her literal "Effacement." The sentence (which at first almost defeats understanding) offers each halting realization slowly, each segment suppressing the realms of animal and vegetable to become purely mineral, each segment answering an unpredictable question that itself stems from the words just uttered and issues in an unpredictable answer generating yet another question:

> "I'm no more your mother than"—
>   than what?
> "than the cloud that"—
>   that does what?
> "distills"—
>   distills what?
> "a mirror to"—
>   to do what?
> "to reflect"—
>   what?
> "its own slow"—
>   slow what?
> "effacement at"—
>   at what?
> "at the wind's"—
>   the wind's what?
> "hand."

As the new mother stumbles along the corridors of this intellectual labyrinth, every expected "natural" foresight in pregnancy of what motherhood has to offer (love, curiosity, nursing, "baby talk") is subtracted; the self-effacement becomes increasingly inorganic, unmammalian. The syntax of this tercet, so peculiar and arresting, displays Plath's talent for saying something—"I don't know where this experience is leading me"—without making the statement explicit. It mimics, in its pacing, the experience itself. A comparable thought-process precedes each of Plath's powerful words in this late phase: "What is it in this phenomenon that makes me call it 'drafty'? What makes it a 'museum'?"

The second half of "Morning Song" takes place some weeks later. The baby has been put to bed, and the maternal ritual of the first sleep-deprived months has begun. The new mother, awakened in the middle of the night by the child's demanding cry (so aggressively different from its soft breathing in sleep), hastens to transfer the baby and its noise into another room. There, while she nurses the child in solitude, the day slowly dawns at the windowpane. Plath, by her title inserting the time of day into the poem, is transforming a known genre. The traditional "morning song"—an *aubade*, from the French *aube,* dawn—shows two lovers in bed, regretting the arrival of the sun (as in Donne's "The Sun Rising"). The baby's open-mouthed hunger-cry modulates over time, as it nurses, into musical cooings of satisfaction, repeated like the notes of a melody. In her startled recognition that the small foreign animal in her arms is now emitting not merely sounds but syllables (vowels and consonants linked into the first phonemes, "ma-ma"), the elated young mother comes to feel that in its possession of even rudimentary language, her baby is another human being like herself. Her spirits rise with the baby's rising notes, and the atmosphere becomes one of festivity, with imaginary birthday balloons.

And that is the plot, a relatively bare one (sketched almost a year after Plath's baby was born), of the speaker's gradual transformation from wife into mother. As the poem opens, the wife (with her husband in attendance) is in her bed at home as the baby is born; she feels for the first time the clash between her former idealizing simile of conception and pregnancy (that love had set in motion a "fat gold watch" inaugurating a golden time)—and the jarrings of childbirth, the midwife's slap and a naked cry. The cry is shockingly perceived as repellently "bald," unadorned, featureless, intimidating. The speaker and her husband fuse to a single "we" at the birth-moment against the baby "you." But in the second half of the poem, the wife leaves the marital bed for the nursing of the child; she becomes (and remains) a single "I," and the husband does not reappear. The marital duo has ceded (at least temporarily) to the maternal one.

PLATH WAS a terribly hardworking poet from her teen years on (as evidenced by her technically fully articulated, if still mostly formulaic, juvenilia). Very early, she had formulated a fully conventional idea of a happy life: she would be a gifted and sexual wife to an exceptional and universally admired husband, and would give birth to many babies (always imagined as babies rather than as children). After her marriage, as soon as she was attempting pregnancy, she raced to find independent imaginative forms for that envisaged life, many of them invented to express in both themes and styles a new, rich, and relatively untreated poetic enterprise: motherhood.

A full year before she had her first child, Plath wrote a single-stanza nine-line (for nine-month) poem entitled "Metaphors," comparing (too archly) the pregnant body to a playful set of equivalents. Each of the nine lines of "Metaphors" has nine syllables, presenting ill-assorted and jesting definitions of the swelling body and its ultimate direction. The pregnant first-person speaker is "An elephant, a ponderous house," and, ridiculously,

"A melon strolling on two tendrils." The last metaphors initiate pregnancy's dangerous momentum: "I've eaten a bag of green apples, / Boarded the train there's no getting off." Too self-conscious and effortful in its casting around for whimsical metaphors, the poem nonetheless is anticipating more work ahead to illuminate motherhood. Less than two months before her child was born, Plath rewrote "Metaphors" into "You're," doubling its size into two stanzas of nine nine-syllabled lines addressed to her fetus (but with the same disorienting overplus of description). One moment the fetus is "Gilled like a fish"; at another it becomes "my little loaf"; at yet another, it reverts to "our traveled prawn," before ultimately becoming "A clean slate." "Metaphors" and "You're," with their incoherence of imagery and artificiality of tone, cannot become interesting poems. A better poem, "Mushrooms," written halfway through pregnancy, does not attempt an individuated embryo, gilled or baked or traveled: instead, it imagines an undifferentiated chorus of half-formed fetuses masquerading metaphorically as speaking mushrooms. They push up irresistibly through loam to air, uttering in tercets (often an "incomplete" form by comparison to couplets or quatrains) their compact two-beat threats of eventual victory:

> Overnight, very
> Whitely, discreetly,
> Very quietly
>
> Our toes, our noses
> Take hold on the loam,
> Acquire the air.

Like fetuses, they require no external feeding: "We //
Diet on water, / On crumbs of shadow." Although they
are initially "meek," they become "Nudgers and shovers /
In spite of ourselves," propelled by genetic force:

> We shall by morning
> Inherit the earth.
> Our foot's in the door.

"Mushrooms" convinces on its own terms, not presuming
on the "human" personality or individuality of the fetus,
but aware that it is unstoppable in its arrival.

It will not be surprising to any reader of Plath that her
youthful imagination, long before it was alerted to preg-
nancy, had specialized in disastrous outcomes (see her
doomsday poems in the juvenilia). Now, with a focus not
global but personal, the dooms become biological. The
anxiety felt during pregnancy by any mother is displaced,
in "Stillborn," onto the writing of poems, as Plath, a few
months into motherhood, finds yet another seam opening
in possible biological sources of poetry. But the elegy for
the stillborn embodies none of the grief a mother would
feel when her expected child does not survive. When
unsuccessful poems become fetuses in formaldehyde,
Plath's brittleness offers a derisive grotesquerie:

> These poems do not live: it's a sad diagnosis.
>
> . . . . .
>
> O I cannot understand what happened to them!
> They are proper in shape and number and every part.
> They sit so nicely in the pickling fluid!

Plath never ceased to explore motherhood, in many poems evoking maternal joy even in tragic contexts. Before I return to that joy, it must be conceded that tragedy had the ultimate victory, and so I glance ahead here to her final visual tableau of maternity, "Edge." It opens with a posthumous tomb-sculpture of a mother and two children, but its second tableau softens to recount the slow hemorrhaging of still-living garden flowers. It is austere in its conviction of the conceptual finality of death, but surprisingly lavish in its gradual farewell to the young bodies of the children. As always in her best poems, Plath's investigation of a topic has both intellectual weight and emotional resonance. In "Edge," the objective, intellectually accurate, immobility of marble "motherhood" coexists with the lamenting heart's mimicry of the gradual dissolution of the body. The chill of the sepulchral group (conveyed in the third person: "The woman is perfected") coexists with the weeping sounds of mourning: "odors bleed / From the sweet, deep throats of the night flower." In a bold move, Plath diminishes her multiple dying flowers to a single one, but the single flower, remembering its past companions, bleeds from multiple throats. Motherhood both is (in sculpture) and is not (in life) eternal.

As "Edge" closes, the spectator looks upward and says, of the indifferent moon, that in the long view of history, "She is used to this sort of thing." Of course she is; history is one long bloodbath. But Plath being Plath, fact and intellect, compelling as they are, are not allotted the last word of the grave-garden. As the spectator looks up from Earth, the moon, humanized, becomes visible as a skeletal hood of bone. But Plath insists on making the moon audible as well, and creates a cold flat music for her witch-cloak: "Her blacks crackle and drag." Plath could not envisage her own death except by making the tomb-sculpture include her children; unless she had her two children with her, she would not be the person she is, but some past self long relinquished. Motherhood is preserved, even after death. "Edge" is an irreproachable poem, but because it memorializes her deathbed self, it belongs thematically with Plath's meditations on death rather than with her poems on living motherhood.

So I turn back here to my central topic—how motherhood allowed Plath to invent a poetics of motherhood—situations, elements, analogies, feelings—and to write sane and joyous poems about and to her children. Although she was never a religious believer, her interest in imaginative emblems of motherhood inevitably led her into the territory of the Christian Nativity myth. The birth of Christ to Mary offered Plath temptations to sharp modern contrasts, of which the most amusing is Plath's playful lyric in which the Magi come to the wrong address. Yeats's magisterial poem "The Magi" might have daunted any successor from appropriating that title, but Plath was bold enough to call her poem, too, "Magi." Yeats's solemn portrayal of "unsatisfied" Magi compelled to return from Calvary to "The uncontrollable mystery on the bestial floor" is comically repudiated in Plath's reimagining of the encounter of a baby girl with such would-be male sponsors.

The scholarly Magi, guided by a moving star, journeyed to greet the Second Person—the Son—of the Holy Trinity of Father, Son, and Holy Spirit. Plath's irony and humorous skepticism mock the idea of wise old men as the best company for a newborn baby. Instead of the biblical gold, frankincense, and myrrh, modern male sponsors in our rational era would bring as gifts to the cradle the Platonic Triad of abstractions: "the Good," "the True," and "the Beautiful." Such philosophical sponsors are a two-dimensional sort of "papery godfolk" who have followed the wrong star to the wrong crib. Because they are looking for a rationalist God, a "lamp-headed Plato," Plath waves them away airily: "What girl ever flourished in such company?" She does not suggest what "company" her baby girl might thrive in. She certainly would need better patrons than the "disquieting Muses" of Plath's own christening, or the star-followers of the Christian story, or the rationalist world's bearers of the Platonic Triad. No invented modern benefactors can fill the gaping absence, and Plath's closing flippancy, though memorable, cannot conceal the lack of suitable protective elders for the modern female baby.

It took a miscarriage and almost a full year of living with her first child to enable Plath to write "Morning Song" for her second. It has many virtues: it does not fall into the sterile unlived jokes of "Metaphors" or into the uneasy repetitions in "You're"; it doesn't impose the Gothic gloom of bottled babies in "Stillborn"; it restrains itself from repeating either reverent biblical mythology or the frustration of Yeats's Magi. Its discipline continues the purity of "Mushrooms," in which, by pluralizing her fetus and reducing it in category from mammal to vegetable, Plath could create an apprehension of threatening organic growth without imposing on her invisible fetus a humanity not yet perceivable. "Morning Song" has the inevitability of birth-momentum—what will happen next once a child is born—but lets the child remain ungendered and unnamed, only a step, one could say, from its fetus-existence.

"Morning Song" hints immediately at biological momentum: the "New statue" utters a "bald cry"—unlovely, unsettling, and insistent, and the first sign of the mother's response to her child is unnervingly intellectual, non-human, as abstract as wind and cloud. That relation, not yet humanized, has its own ongoing momentum, as distillation effects effacement. Surely this is the most detached portrait of motherhood in literature. Without the strangeness of its first three stanzas, "Morning Song" could not have gained the measured steps into love by which it progresses, never putting a foot wrong in its steady pace.

Just as ontogeny recapitulates phylogeny in "You're" (in which the fetus has gills as it goes about becoming human), so motherhood in "Morning Song" begins its metaphors for the baby in the strange realm of a remote insect-species as the child produces its "moth-breath." (Alliteration at the end of a word rather than the beginning—"moth/breath"—although almost invisible, is one sound-connection that often gives Plath's poetry an unusual texture.) At the next level of being, the "New statue" has now advanced in species from insect to animal, uttering an urgent cry from a mouth like a cat's; the cry produces a companion animal, a "cow-heavy" lactating mother. The mother's swift removal of the child and herself into another room takes a further step—the grounding of the "I" of the mother in a physiological function, nursing, that is impossible to the male. The collective "we" of the couple never returns after the double establishment of the female "I"—first in the abstract terms of "I'm no more your mother" and second in the down-to-earth self-description by the young woman: "One cry, and I stumble from bed, cow-heavy." The inalterable momentum of the cosmos (the cloud, the effacing wind) creates the rising dawn that "swallows" the night stars, past selves, as they dull after the irrevocable change of motherhood. The penultimate moment of the poem—in which the child, choosing its "notes," becomes a human creature of intentional melody—arrives prefaced by the traditional *Et iam* remembered from the Latin poets, the "And now" that lifts an ongoing temporal curve into the present. Plath may be remembering Keats's closing of his autumn ode:

>and now . . .
>The red-breast whistles from a garden-croft;
>And gathering swallows twitter in the skies.

The completeness implied in the conventional endpoint—"And now"—wraps mother and baby and reader in the ecstatic moment in which the baby becomes human, the mother perceives the first sign of communication, and the reader feels the lift of the mother's imagined balloons.

It was the impeccable constancy of pace that moved me when I first read "Morning Song": everything now on its way, the sequence of phases confident, the ending happy—not triumphant like the victory of those mushroom-invaders, but mutual, intelligible, reassuring. Later, as I saw further into the poem, its shadows troubled me: the permanent vanishing of the husband; the disappearance of the marital "we" in favor of the maternal "I"; the severe apprehension of personal effacement by the very decision to give birth; the permanence of universal natural "elements" of inorganic and organic existence (cloud, wind, birth, cry, nourishment, mind, death) within the swift transience of a single life from birth to the sepulcher;

the conceptual incompatibility of abstractions (cloud, mirror, wind) and individuals (mother and infant).

My first emotional and structural responses to "Morning Song" did not yet admit me into Plath's subtlety of sound, her claim on our subliminal response to the phonetic transfusion of the poem even as we gather the plot, the architecture, the pacing, and climax (or climaxes) as we traverse it. I hadn't at first seen that the "moth-breath" was so styled because it reproduced part of the word "mother," or that "mirror" echoed "mother" in rhythm and length as well as in sound. "Midwife," "mother," and "mirror," all trochees (with stressed/unstressed rhythms), fit together as a birth-trinity; the cosmic wind's invisible "hand" condenses itself into the audible "handful" of notes. Even the changes of agent in the closing lines make a container for the reader's sense of closing events. We look in different directions—north, south, east, west—as the human gives way to the non-human: the organic dyad of mother and baby disappears into the inorganic dyad of window and dawn; the organic living body of the child produces the inorganic "notes" and "vowels." Only a very flexible mind can hold in a single instant a whitening window swallowing stars, a baby's proffering of melodic notes, and a mother's vision of phonemic sound-balloons defined by their vowels. The "thickness" of such coalescences gives weight and solidity to Plath's conclusion, bestows on the "New statue" an earned animation, and prompts in the new mother an awakening of love.

Plath's meditations on motherhood continue to deepen, enabling the reach and success of "Parliament Hill Fields," a poem written when Plath suffered a miscarriage less than a year after her daughter Frieda's birth. For the poem, Plath invents a yes-no structure replicating the existence/nonexistence of the fetus as it bleeds out, and replicating the movement of thought as well, as it returns repeatedly to a trauma. She interrupts her verse-narrative in this way with sad but stoic addresses to the never-to-be-known fetus:

> Your absence is inconspicuous;
> Nobody can tell what I lack.
>
> . . . . .
>
> I suppose it's pointless to think of you at all.
> Already your doll grip lets go.
>
> . . . . .
>
> Your cry fades like the cry of a gnat.
> I lose sight of you on your blind journey[.]
>
> . . . . .
>
> The day empties its images
> Like a cup or a room.

The day discards its hopes as the womb discards its burden. For consolation, Plath reminds herself that she has a living daughter at home, and summons up, as she walks, the glow-in-the-dark picture on the nursery wall. One by one, in her imagination, the objects in the picture begin to reveal their colors, but as Plath tries to install haloed angel-presences, each image collapses into transparent falsity; each "Blue shrub behind the glass // Exhales an indigo nimbus, / A sort of cellophane balloon." She returns home apprehensively: "The old dregs, the old difficulties take me to wife."

It was only a week after that depressed requiem for a miscarriage that Plath turned to the past and wrote "Morning Song" for comfort, but its closing joy took on weight, I believe, through her continuing sorrow over the lost pregnancy. The instability of her mood is such that two days after writing "Morning Song" (February 19), Plath's mind, meditating on motherhood, raises two unnerving specters: she composes "Barren Woman" (February 21), reflecting her fear of infertility, and its parallel "Heavy Women" (February 26), about disillusion after childbirth. The pregnant women "Smiling to themselves" and "beautifully smug" await birth in an ominous landscape where "the axle of winter / Grinds round, bearing down with the straw, / The star, the wise grey men." "Bearing down," the women will experience grinding tragedy as an inevitable consequence of giving birth.

Plath had thought that her life would offer, as sources of joy, the rich aesthetic stimuli of conception, pregnancy, and motherhood, and after her miscarriage her imagination clung to those stimuli even as suicide (presided over by a funereal yew-tree and a moon "With the O-gape of complete despair") rises into competition with them.

ALTHOUGH IT is true that Plath's suicidal depression and the violent poems that it produced won her fame, the tragic evidence of her mental illness has so dominated anthologies that her efforts to record and express joy tend to recede out of sight. Except for "Morning Song," the selections from Plath's poetry in *The Norton Anthology of Poetry* introduce readers solely to the grim Plath, each poem bearing its portrait of ruin:

"I crawl like an ant in mourning" ("The Colossus")

"The tulips should be behind bars like dangerous animals" ("Tulips")

"I have suffered the atrocity of sunsets." ("Elm")

"If I've killed one man, I've killed two——" ("Daddy")

"The dew that flies / Suicidal" ("Ariel")

"I rise with my red hair / And I eat men like air."
("Lady Lazarus")

But as Plath, with her acute ear, completed and disciplined experience into form, the work of analysis permitted her an impersonal joy in creation that inspires even in her tragic poems an inescapable vitality. Even when Plath cannot maintain her joy in motherhood, even when a menacing darkness encroaches upon the child, the initial hope and joy appear and reappear in Plath's lines.

"Nick and the Candlestick" begins in a sunless underground cave, lit by a single candle. We see Plath transform the hellish cave into a place beautiful enough to house her beloved new child, Nicholas. The vowel-sound of the word "love," touch by touch ("Love, love," "hung," "rugs," "of"), decorates the space of the poem, while alliterations ("roses," "rugs," "Victoriana") link the images:

> Love, love,
> I have hung our cave with roses,
> With soft rugs——
>
> The last of Victoriana.

Excoriating "the mercuric / Atoms that cripple," Plath confirms to her son the cosmic new era produced by his birth:

> You are the one
> Solid the spaces lean on, envious.
> You are the baby in the barn.

Still, the secularized parallel with the birth of Christ weakens, rather than strengthens, the poem. To demonstrate the inspiration that Plath found when she turned her gaze to motherhood (as well as her anticipatory guilt as she planned her death), there is no better illustration than "Child," where even her hyperboles turn tranquil:

> Your clear eye is the one absolutely beautiful thing.
> I want to fill it with color and ducks,
> The zoo of the new
>
> Whose names you meditate—
> April snowdrop, Indian pipe,
> Little
>
> Stalk without wrinkle,
> Pool in which images
> Should be grand and classical
>
> Not this troublous
> Wringing of hands, this dark
> Ceiling without a star.

Plath could include the joy of "Child" at the same time as she was foretelling her death in "Edge." The longer she lived, the more inextricable the alternate truths became.

There were, and are, many difficulties in inventing poems transmitting the labile emotions surrounding the birth of children. As Plath's efforts suggest, it is hardest of all to attach poems to pregnancy when it is uneventful: while the cells are merely multiplying, no intellectual cause wakes the imagination. When Plath treats only the physiological events, the poems ("Metaphors," for example) are unfruitful; as soon as there is an emotional event (a miscarriage, say) the poems reach fullness and credibility. Since so much of the biology of fertility is routine, biology alone cannot provide subjects for poems. Lived responses to motherhood—because there is so little access to them in the poetry of the past, and because biology itself seemed fatally governed by that indifferent moon of the impersonal universe—have not been easy to galvanize into poetry. But Plath had courage: even when life seemed meaningless, she actively sought out new genres of childbirth and motherhood (a miscarriage poem, a Thalidomide poem, a posthumous poem).

What medicine had to offer Plath—electroshock, inefficient medications, "talk therapy"—was too little. (A few years after Plath's death, Robert Lowell began treatment with lithium, which, for all its drawbacks, enabled him to live.) Plath, who studied with Lowell, admitted her debt to his autobiographical *Life Studies*, but their styles distinguished them—his, ever more forcefully adjectival and "plotted," hers, more surreal and fanciful and excited (she had a weakness for exclamation marks, which she vigorously deleted in revision). "Language" that "adds to the stock of available reality"—R. P. Blackmur's definition of the purpose of poetry— requires the day-by-day courage to devise an individual style, which issues from a strongly individual sensibility inseparable from a desire to play with language. (Pound defined poetry as "the dance of the intellect among words.") In Plath's *Unabridged Journals*, published in 2000, thirty-seven years after her death, we follow, with pity and confusion, the incessant nightmares and tormenting emotions of an incurable patient hurled hither and yon by episodes of insanity. But from those chaotic journal pages, Plath somehow, by a perfectionism of instinct and intellect, drew her painstaking and commanding map of madness—madness disciplined, made strikingly euphonious, rhythmic, plotted, and controlled.

In the *Journals* during periods of illness, she is baffled, hysterical, malicious, vengeful, paranoid, frightened, self-loathing, and lonely beyond belief; and on the other hand, at her less anguished moments she is boastful, idealistic, hardworking, vain, self-congratulatory, self-sacrificing, resolute, and—in her best and sanest moods—tender, kind, and loving. She had an eye that noticed the smallest details of life, and her poems of motherhood are full of them: who else would say of motherhood (as she does in "Thalidomide"): "All night I carpenter // A space for the thing I am given, / A love // Of two wet eyes and a screech." In her poems of motherhood, her highly colored lines strive constantly for truth, irony, comedy, and wit before they are bleached out by death.

The paucity of convincing poems about motherhood remains evident. Few people are educated to the level needed to write original verse. (Most of the great English lyrics came from writers who knew several languages, usually including Latin, were beset by imagination, had a keen sense of poetic genres, were delighted by etymology, had read hundreds of fine poems and knew many of those by heart, and possessed an instinctive ear for cadence. The autodidacts—Clare and Blake in England, Whitman and Dickinson in America—taught themselves by reading intensely, not least the Bible and Shakespeare, and often by loving another art; see Whitman on "the trained soprano" and Dickinson on "The fascinating chill that Music leaves.") Few women writers become mothers; and too few mothers have the time, energy, money, and talent to write works of genius. Successful women writers have been, for the most part, single, protected, and rich. Too late for the eras of patronage and too early for reliable birth control, many talented women gave up creative hopes.

Plath did have a patron—a wealthy woman novelist named Olive Higgins Prouty—and she grew up in a house full of books, the child of two teachers. But the familial heritage of depression proved a lethal one. Plath's father Otto refused for four years to be examined or treated for an illness that he insisted was lung cancer but that was actually treatable diabetes; Sylvia, by her own account, felt that she died when her father did, and first attempted suicide (almost successfully) at twenty, then gassed herself at thirty; and her son Nicholas—"the baby in the barn"— after years of depression, hanged himself at forty-seven. The darkness finally defeated, too early, the gifts even of this first adequate and observant poet of motherhood.

The Selfless Self of Self

On the Portrait of Two Beautiful Young People

  a Brother and Sister

O I admire and sorrow! The heart's eye grieves
Discovering you, dark tramplers, tyrant years.
A juice rides rich through bluebells, in vine leaves,
And beauty's dearest veriest vein is tears.

Happy the father, mother of these! Too fast:
Not that, but thus far, all with frailty, blest
In one fair fall; but, for time's aftercast,
Creatures all heft, hope, hazard, interest.

And are they thus? The fine, the fingering beams
Their young delightful hour do feature down
That fleeted else like day-dissolvèd dreams
Or ringlet-race on burling Barrow brown.

She leans on him with such contentment fond
As well the sister sits, would well the wife;
His looks, the soul's own letters, see beyond,
Gaze on, and fall directly forth on life.

But ah, bright forelock, cluster that you are
Of favoured make and mind and health and youth,
Where lies your landmark, seamark, or soul's star?
There's none but truth can stead you. Christ is truth.

There's none but good can bé good, both for you
And what sways with you, maybe this sweet maid;
None good but God—a warning wavèd to
One once that was found wanting when Good weighed.

Man lives that list, that leaning in the will
No wisdom can forecast by gauge or guess,
The selfless self of self, most strange, most still,
Fast furled and all foredrawn to No or Yes.

Your feast of; that most in you earnest eye
May but call on your banes to more carouse.
Worst will the best. What worm was here, we cry,
To have havoc-pocked so, see, the hung-heavenward
    boughs?

Enough: corruption was the world's first woe.
What need I strain my heart beyond my ken?
O but I bear my burning witness though
Against the wild and wanton work of men.

                        GERARD MANLEY HOPKINS

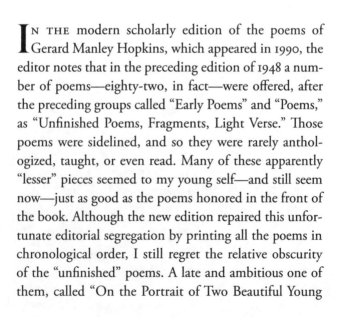

IN THE modern scholarly edition of the poems of
Gerard Manley Hopkins, which appeared in 1990, the
editor notes that in the preceding edition of 1948 a num-
ber of poems—eighty-two, in fact—were offered, after
the preceding groups called "Early Poems" and "Poems,"
as "Unfinished Poems, Fragments, Light Verse." Those
poems were sidelined, and so they were rarely anthol-
ogized, taught, or even read. Many of these apparently
"lesser" pieces seemed to my young self—and still seem
now—just as good as the poems honored in the front of
the book. Although the new edition repaired this unfor-
tunate editorial segregation by printing all the poems in
chronological order, I still regret the relative obscurity
of the "unfinished" poems. A late and ambitious one of
them, called "On the Portrait of Two Beautiful Young

People," is worth pondering, not least to draw readers' attention to its existence. It embodies the agony of Hopkins's last years, in which he repeatedly staged a debate between his own theory of unbidden creativity and the religious theory of free will.

At the age of twenty-two, Gerard Hopkins, an ardent young English poet and a recent graduate of Oxford (where he had shone as a brilliant student of the classics), prays that he may willingly advance beyond the legitimate pleasures of the senses in favor of the better joys of ascetic devotion. For the delight of the ear in song and speech, he will substitute contemplative silence and muteness in self-expression; instead of the distractions of worldly life, his eye will "find the uncreated light." In gentle and unstrained "perfect" quatrains, each rhythmically serene line rhyming exactly with another, he enjoins the five natural senses to fix on spiritual pleasures. He begins the poem which he calls "The Habit of Perfection" with the ear and the eye:

> Elected Silence, sing to me
> And beat upon my whorlèd ear,
> Pipe me to pastures still and be
> The music that I care to hear.
>
> Shape nothing, lips; be lovely-dumb:
> It is the shut, the curfew sent
> From there where all surrenders come
> Which only makes you eloquent.
>
> Be shellèd, eyes, with double dark
> And find the uncreated light:
> This ruck and reel which you remark
> Coils, keeps, and teases simple sight.

He burned his own copies of his youthful poems (leaving some copies, however, with family and friends and letting others remain in drafts embedded in his diaries). Then, converted from his family's Anglican Protestantism to Roman Catholicism, Gerard Hopkins became a Jesuit priest.

He had supposed, before his ordination, that his ascetic desire to disregard sense-pleasure would ensure access to higher spiritual delights, and that he would willingly suspend his writing of poems in favor of consecrating all his time to his priestly duties. He did just that for seven years. Then, with the implied permission (or so he felt) of his Jesuit superior, who had said that someone should commemorate the five German Roman Catholic nuns, legally expelled from Germany for their religion, who had drowned when their ship, the *Deutschland*, was wrecked off the coast of Kent, Hopkins resumed writing poetry with a fiercely original long poem called "The Wreck of the Deutschland." Hopkins's return to the practice of verse continued until his premature death, of typhoid fever, when he was only forty-four.

After his untroubled and openhearted early election of silence, now writing as a priest, Hopkins became troubled by an increasingly anxious scrupulosity, suspecting that art must be blighted in its essence, infected by that original sin inherited by all human beings. If he, vowed to God's service, chooses to write poetry, does he sin by that worldly choice? In an extraordinarily agile swerve, Hopkins rebukes, in the draft of a poem, the idea that composing a work of art—whether architectural or musical—is rightly characterized as an act of free will subject to moral judgment, arguing that the artist is driven to create by a compelling force subject to no external law, divine or secular. (The untitled draft which we used to know by its first line "How all's to one thing wrought!," has had its stanzas rearranged, and the first line now reads "Who shaped these walls has shewn." The rearrangement seems to me unconvincing.) It is impossible, he believes, to deduce the moral state of the artist or the composer from the work of art, since art is not created on a plane to which the moral law applies. The concept of obedience to a preexisting moral or spiritual law and the concept of the freedom of the will are simply not relevant to the surprising and unpremeditated surge of inspiration which arises spontaneously, unbidden by the will.

Drawing on his own experience, Hopkins claims that the artist is moved by a strange controlling power:

> Not free in this because
> His powers seemed free to play:
> He swept that scope he was
> To sweep and must obey.
>
> Nor angel insight can
> Learn how the heart is hence:
> Since all the make of man
> Is law's indifference.
>
> Therefóre this masterhood,
> This piece of perfect song,
> This fault-not-found-with good
> Is neither right nor wrong.

Stung by the frequent condemnation of artworks (and, by implication, of artists) on moral grounds, Hopkins dismisses such judgments by giving to his unphilosophical reader—in absolutely plain, even childish, language—examples of three arts that cannot possibly be evaluated by moral standards: painting, melody, and the "architectural" constructions (such as a honeycomb) of animal instinct. These are "neither right nor wrong,"

> No more than red and blue,
> No more than Re and Mi,
> Or sweet the golden glue
> That's built for by the bee.

Clever as this is, it has not come to grips with the semantic content of the poet's own poems: must they, because their medium is language, exist on the human plane of right and wrong, conforming themselves to a binary ethic of Yes or No? Or can his poems be left to exist solely on the aesthetic plane from which they originated, where the criterion of success is the approach to formal perfection? In judging art, must we abandon the aesthetic of the working artist, where inspiration drives what Keats called "the innumerable compositions and decompositions" intrinsic to the task of writing poetry? May the artist not conceive of his works as belonging among the pure "wild and wide" goods of Nature, all divinely created, all of innumerable shadings?

> For good grows wild and wide,
> Has shades, is nowhere none;

Or must he instead value his poetry according to its (cruelly restricted) choice of a single presiding ethical "chieftain," God or Satan?

> But right must seek a side
> And choose for chieftain one.

Is the purpose of art to achieve a compelled artifact aspiring to perfection of form? Or is it rather to present a substantial moral argument? At this moment in his intellectual evolution, Hopkins offers an enigmatic two-part answer:

> What makes the man and what
> The man within that makes:
> Ask whom he serves or not
> Serves and what side he takes.

The poet's riddle asks first "What makes the man" (to which the answer is presumably a natural process, since the poet is not asking "Who makes the man"). Even more strangely, the riddle in its next two lines asks about the verse-product, about "what / The man within that makes." What is the context, the "that" which the man is "within"? By its neutral reference, "that" must once again stand for a natural process. In his four-line epigram Hopkins sums up the apparently impersonal natural force impelling the human creator, no less a creature of biological instinct than the bee. Only after asserting the idiosyncratic force that both makes and is made by the artist can the poet raise the question of the artist's ultimate moral allegiance. When Hopkins stations against each other the natural, passionate, and independent urgency of creation and the strict moral urgency of intellectually ethical decision, the riddling relation between the two urgencies is an uneasy one.

SEVEN YEARS pass. It is 1886 and Hopkins is forty-two. Everything has changed in his circumstances: in 1884 he had been dispatched from England to Ireland to serve as Professor of Classics in the Catholic University in Dublin, newly refounded by the Jesuits. Remembering, painfully, Jesus's announcement "I came not to send peace, but a sword" (Matthew 10:34), the poet finds himself isolated "at three removes," not only from his native England but also from his Protestant family and his former company of English Jesuits. In a post-famine era when Ireland was implacably hostile to England, he was the only English Jesuit in all of Ireland. He realizes, desolately, that his university appointment in Dublin is likely to be permanent:

> To seem the stranger lies my lot, my life
> Among strangers. Father and mother dear,
> Brothers and sisters are in Christ not near
> And he my peace / my parting, sword and strife.
> . . . . .
>
> I am in Ireland now; now I am at a third
> Remove.

His depression is so intense that he refers to himself in the past tense, as though he had died: he is not a "beginner" but "a lonely began."

The religious, intellectual, scholarly, psychological, and physical trials that Hopkins had undergone in Ireland brought him, in 1886, the year of his poem on the portrait of two beautiful children, to a crisis of distress in which his commitment to accuracy obliged him to graph, in a meticulous and experimental style, his mind's unbearable nervous oscillations among countless possible thoughts. His aesthetic drive is increasingly conditioned by a merciless self-scrutiny, the "helpless self-loathing" that he reveals in his later Dublin retreat notes. His familiar but ever-changing standoff between the aesthetic and the moral now reappears in a tense poem that he names as if it were a commentary: "On the Portrait of Two Beautiful Young People." When he sees, presumably in a wealthy family's house, a watercolor portrait of two children, he is on his Christmas holiday. He has found it almost impossible to write poetry while teaching, but with his incessant anxiety somewhat reduced by distance from the university, he has the freedom to admire the art of the portraitist as well as the appealing beauty of the children. His title renders them merely as ungendered young people, but his subtitle ("a Brother and Sister") represents them as preadolescent siblings, their innocence still undamaged.

Although the poet's initial response is an admiring one, ratifying the double beauty of both the children and the tender portrait, his anxiety soon awakens reflection on the children, their parents, and their probable future, and his mind leaps to an immediate moral sorrow inseparable from his initial aesthetic admiration. "O I admire," he says while attaching—without taking a breath—his second verb and its exclamation point, "and sorrow!" In that first line, he establishes the rapid—the instantaneous—fluctuations of response that the poem will mirror. His mixed emotions sometimes arrive in balanced opposition, but more often they emerge as restless questioning, philosophical perplexity, or psychological dread. Compared with the tranquility of "Elected Silence" in "The Habit of Perfection," the turbulent stirrings besetting him before the portrait allow him only temporary moments of repose, each one rapidly disturbed into further disquiet. The tide of admiration that had in the past prompted "How all's to one thing wrought!" ebbs, undermined by the looming sorrow prompted by the portrait.

Hopkins's increasing depression will bring him, by the end of the poem, to a desperate conclusion—that destiny may destroy these children. In that respect, the "beautiful" but static watercolor is mendacious. The artist has framed the children within a wreath of unspoiled flowers, fruit on tree-branches, and flourishing grapevines (generating the "bluebells" and "juice" of the first stanza), but does this unblemished context truthfully reflect the variable and endangered course of human fate that must be undergone by the children? Remembering the tree of the knowledge of good and evil from which Eve, tempted by the serpent, plucked the forbidden fruit, the poet arrives, in his penultimate stanza, at a dire image of the children's likely future, crying out, as he approaches his conclusion, against the fall of man that brought disease and death into the world:

> What worm was here, we cry,
> To have havoc-pocked so, see, the hung-heavenward
>   boughs?

As Hopkins mentioned in a letter, he adopted as his verse-form the sedate, if sorrowful, perfectly rhymed quatrains of Gray's famous "Elegy Written in a Country Churchyard" because he thought that he could "make something." He, too, is writing an elegy grieving the children's potential end, likely to be a blighted one. Six years earlier, responding to the tears of the child "Margaret" mourning the fall of leaves, he had expressed a horrible certainty with the words "born for": "It is the blight man was born for, / It is Margaret you mourn for." At least

Gray could predict the certain future of his dead villagers: they will be recalled, if at all, in "The short and simple annals of the poor." Their humble life, while it may exclude the prospect of political or literary fame, also keeps them from the hideous criminal acts of the powerful: they will not "wade through slaughter to a throne, / And shut the gates of mercy on mankind." Hopkins, by contrast, can say nothing so reassuring about the children: his fear disrupts his lines, hurling them far from Gray's even pace and calm punctuation. Both the poet's quandary before the mendacious (and therefore sentimental) portrait—representing life falsely as a paradisal scene—and his vexing ignorance of the children's moral future obliterate tranquility as soon as the poem opens.

Hopkins's emotional announcement—"O I admire and sorrow!"—had burst forth, forcibly breaking its single line in two by the word "sorrow" and the full stop at the exclamation point. The second stanza—Hopkins's unsettling transcription of his almost simultaneous mental self-contradictions—presents, as its mimicry of agitated thought, an unstable and incoherent syntax and an oversupply of punctuation (nine commas, an exclamation point, a colon, a semicolon, a period). We could paraphrase the stanza and iron out our first impressions of incoherence by following Hopkins's line of reasoning: we could say that Hopkins first exclaims how happy the parents are in having such beautiful children, then feels that he spoke too quickly. No, he stammers, the parents cannot be said to be permanently happy (that particular luck cannot be ensured); but at least the parents are happy thus far, but we must recall (he reluctantly admits) the frailty of fortune; and after the present fleeting phase of childhood there will be an "aftercast" of time's baleful dice—with what result? Following that gamble, the children's fate and its effect on their parents can only be speculated upon. These young creatures are to their parents, thinks the poet in summary, a "heft" (a burden, from "heave"), a "hope," a "hazard" (all alliterating with, and thereby reinforcing, the initial "Happy"). Yet in the final noun, they become merely an "interest." This, the sole "neutral" noun of the series, detaches the spectator Hopkins from his initial emotional participation in the "Happy" parents' good fortune.

If we consider, now, our first glimpse of this second stanza, we see Hopkins—hardly yet into his subject— becoming almost unintelligible as he daringly mimics on the page the confusing and reckless speed of his turbulent thought:

> Happy the father, mother of these! Too fast:
> Not that, but thus far, all with frailty, blest
> In one fair fall; but, for time's aftercast,
> Creatures all heft, hope, hazard, interest.

Hopkins will continue to represent the very melody of his mind's oscillations in distress: these sometimes appear in balanced oppositions but more often become percussive in restless questioning, philosophical perplexity, or further dread. His music culminates in a broken syntax and ill-coupled words as he addresses one of the endangered and innocent siblings, the brother, approaching (the poet fears) that almost certain ruined end:

> Your feast of; that most in you earnest eye
> May but call on your banes to more carouse.

Worst will the best. What worm was here, we cry,
To have havoc-pocked so, see, the hung-heavenward
    boughs?

As the poem reaches its deepest image, which had been
lurking in the poem from the opening, the words careen
from zenith to pit, from pit to zenith. First Hopkins
announces the benign "feast," reflecting the boy's earnest
and innocent eye, but the feast immediately generates (in
forward linear time) the gluttonous "carouse" of agents
of ruin. By contrast, the next two examples are grimly
retrospective: the outcome ("Worst") is prophesied of its
beautiful past counter-superlative "best," and behind the
disastrous "havoc-pocked" branches we glimpse the orig-
inally healthy "hung-heavenward boughs." The passion-
ate indignation behind such retrospective truth declares
itself in this disequilibrium of time, as it goes forward and
backward in depicting hope succeeded by despair. (Hop-
kins must have noticed, as a schoolboy, the originality of
Shakespeare's pre-positioned disasters in lines where time
has already dealt a death-blow before we are allowed to see
the charm of youth, and time is already digging the grave
of a fair countenance: "Time doth transfix the flourish set
on youth, / And delves the parallels in beauty's brow.")
    Against the buffets of threatening speculation, Hopkins
allows occasional points of repose. The first is his initial
admiring gaze on the tableau of the quiet and lovely por-
trait, where the artist has wreathed the beautiful siblings
in a cluster of unspoiled flowers and grapevine, generat-
ing the bluebells, vine leaves, and juice of the first stanza.
But that initial pleasure is destroyed as soon as "sorrow"
transfixes "admire," "tyrant years" obliterate "youth," and

"tears" mar "beauty." In the second instance in which anxiety is momentarily stilled, the poet creates in fantasy a serene future portrait where a conjectured young wife would replace the sister now by the boy's side, while the boy himself, with the passage of time a husband, is poised (unlike his conditionally inserted bride) in a present-tense future, looking with steadfast confidence to his coming life:

> She leans on him with such contentment fond
> As well the sister sits, would well the wife;
> His looks, the soul's own letters, see beyond,
> Gaze on, and fall directly forth on life.

Yet even in the poised moment of that imagined marriage portrait, the poet's intellectual skepticism speaks out, warning the promising boy that he must embark on a moral and spiritual search for a reliable principle of stability:

> But ah, bright forelock, cluster that you are
> Of favoured make and mind and health and youth,
> Where lies your landmark, seamark, or soul's star?
> There's none but truth can stead you. Christ is truth.

In this direct address, echo-words create deliberate shadow-appearances of earlier poems. The first two echo-words, "mark," and "star," recall Shakespeare's saying of love,

> it is an ever-fixèd mark
> That looks on tempests and is never shaken;
> It is the star to every wand'ring bark[.]

Shakespeare's "ever-fixèd mark" is (to Hopkins's mind) a landmark, a lighthouse, and his star is the North Star by which sailors can navigate. The third echo-word here is "stead," creating a shadow-appearance of Keats's praise of the North Star in the sonnet "Bright star, would I were stedfast as thou art." That line supplies, with its adjective "ste[a]dfast," Hopkins's "archaic" (*OED*) verb, "to stead" (to support, to help), for his desired outcome—that something will "stead" the boy in consistent uprightness as he advances in time.

Having asked the question of where lies that which will "stead" the boy, Hopkins offers, in a startling turn, two different and independent answers: "There's none but truth can stead you. Christ is truth." Each of the two answers in the line occupies a freestanding sentence utter-ing a single thought; each exhibits an unequivocal clos-ing period; and each exists on its own distinct plane. The planes do not intersect. The first sentence replicates the poet's instant answer to his own question on the plane of moral philosophy: "There's none but truth can stead you." The second sentence, "Christ is truth," astonish-ingly inserts itself into the very same line-unit as the first, even though it exists on an entirely different level, that of Christian scripture. The first sentence sets before the boy's eyes a daily intellectual and moral value—truth—indis-pensable to Hopkins himself, as his letters fiercely show. Yet the second, a scriptural sentence, "Christ is truth," echoes Jesus's saying: "I am the way, the truth, and the life" (John 14:6). Such a credal assertion is less universally applicable than the common recommendation of moral truth as a reliable bulwark of the virtuous life.

To be true to himself, Hopkins has had to separate his two truths—one natural, one theological—and give to each its independence. Yet to present himself as he is, the poet has had to twin the two independent answers within a single line, as permanent absolute values equally held by him, inseparable. The poem balances precariously over the abyss between the two absolute standards, philosophical and theological. As he stands immobilized between the two distinct truths, Hopkins's anxious mind, worrying for the young boy, hopes to bridge the abyss with a moral parable from a scriptural source: Jesus's parable of the rich young man. There, invoking a value—the "Good"—that is apparently more flexible than "truth" and of a wider application, Hopkins creates another temporary point of mental repose, but blights it by recounting the biblical parable's unhappy conclusion.

In the brief parable, a rich young man, addressing Jesus as "Good Master," asks what he must do to be saved. After rebuking him for the flattering title ("there is none good but one, that is, God"), Jesus tells the young man to observe the commandments. When the young man, professing that he has obeyed the commandments from his youth, asks what he must further do to be saved, Jesus offers a direct two-part answer: "go and sell that thou hast, and give to the poor . . . and come and follow me." The evangelist recounts the failed outcome: the young man "went away sorrowful: for he had great possessions" (Matthew 19:16–22). In Hopkins's poem, the young man "was found wanting when Good weighed." Knowing that the young people in the portrait are rich, Hopkins hopes to "stead" them by recalling to their minds Jesus's warning that there is none good but God; he also reminds them that the young man was found wanting when he could not imagine depriving himself of riches. (A discarded stanza tells us that the poet forecasts a similar potential sin in the children, saying to them of the young man, "rise he could not; fell / Rather: he wore that millstone you wear, wealth.")

So far, the poet's forensic move in recommending truth has been to direct the boy to three different sources of truth—philosophical, credal, and parabolic. Unsatisfied with all three, Hopkins takes refuge in another source entirely, one existing on a plane unknown to his initial three. In one of the moves that made readers of the first edition of Hopkins's poems in 1918 find him excitingly "modern," the poet's mind leaps to a psychological plane, a trustworthy source to "stead" the boy's future. This resource, very obliquely described, has already been hinted at in one stanza of "How all's to one thing wrought!" Although the artist there, said Hopkins, "changed in choice," he did so not freely but compelled by "his being's bent": that "bent" "was an instrument / Which overvaulted voice." The voice must follow, in every moment of choice, the "being's bent," the innate inclination of the self-being of the artist. In this way, the poet of "On the Portrait" leaps, in the climax of his poem, to the plane of the unfathomable, surpassing the three earlier recommendations—moral, credal, and scriptural. All three, after all, are conventional and well-known to Christian homiletics. But now—on the analogy of his lingering Anglican belief in predestination—that God has decided from all eternity who will be saved and who will be damned, Hopkins has conceived a psychological plane of predestined idiosyncratic selfhood.

Somewhere inside the person, inside the very self, there is a preplanted banner of the inaccessible source within the self. The banner remains in an inscrutable furled form which hides its emblem of "The selfless self of self"—an abstraction unnamable as self or soul because it precedes both, resembling the Aristotelian "form" that determines a distinctive species-nature within inert earthly matter. For Hopkins, it was a matter of introspective fact that not only did each individual species differ from every other species, but every individual human being differed entirely from every other individual being, each bound, when engaged aesthetically, to express itself as itself. In the sonnet "As kingfishers catch fire," Hopkins writes the poem of that conviction:

> Each mortal thing does one thing and the same:
> Deals out that being indoors each one dwells;
> Selves—goes its self; *myself* it speaks and spells,
> Crying *What I do is me: for that I came.*
>
> I say more: the just man justices[.]

As he says in a notebook, he finds his self-being both distinctive and incommunicable: "my selfbeing, . . . that taste of myself, of *I* and *me* above and in all things . . . is more distinctive than the taste of ale or alum, more distinctive than the smell of walnutleaf or camphor, and is incommunicable by any means to another man." At its deepest, his self-being was inaccessible even to the poet himself; otherwise he would have been able to find words to communicate it to others. Instead, he knows it only as the region from which the bolt of inspiration arrives, not at his summoning but as a gift. (Before Freud speculated on the incessant activity of the unconscious mind, insights were felt to be bestowed, not self-generated.)

FROM THE outset of "On the Portrait of Two Beautiful Young People," the poet's linguistic patterns have attempted to arrange themselves under the broad concepts of "authentic" and "inauthentic" (on the aesthetic plane) and "good" and "evil" (on the moral plane). The mounting mass of words of uncertainty in the poem, amid its repeated stops and starts of syntax and punctuation, undoes the overt emotional contrast of admiration and sorrow with which the poet had begun. In short, the aesthetic aim of "On the Portrait of Two Beautiful Young People" is to mimic, credibly, the poet's unpredictable vicissitudes of response as he perceives, from the angle of experience, the precarious future of innocence—by no means an unknown theme in previous verse, but rarely found, as here, in a single extended panicked struggle. The mind here, as it thinks one thing, instantly thinks its opposite, or else it cannot find clear opposites, or it is sunk in prophetic conflict, or it is about to relinquish altogether any attempt at coherence. In earlier verse, experience, modeled on religious conviction, tended to judge firmly: think of Blake's "Auguries of Innocence," with their instant condemnations and approvals: "A Robin Red breast in a Cage / Puts all Heaven in a Rage"; "If the Sun & Moon should Doubt, / Theyd immediately Go out." Hopkins's intellectual subtlety instantly raises not one judgment, but all possible ones, but his love of truth makes him abhor his own skepticism.

As Hopkins suffers through his meditation on the portrait, he has seen the future of the children threatened by agents that could blight their branches of bright leaves and fruit. The worm—at once the serpent of the Fall of Man and Shakespeare's canker-worm in the rose—devours the optimism of the poet's initial hope, and deprives him, by the time his lyric ends, of all notes but tragedy and fury:

> Enough: corruption was the world's first woe.
> What need I strain my heart beyond my ken?
> O but I bear my burning witness though
> Against the wild and wanton work of men.

In the fair copy that Hopkins sent to his friend Robert Bridges, the poem "On the Portrait" ends there, but Hopkins showed that he hoped to add more by appending two lines of asterisks before he mailed it off for Bridges's scrutiny. Nowhere does he explain the function of "The selfless self of self," and how it fits, or does not, with the triple recommendations of truth preceding it.

"How all's to one thing wrought!" had been spoken from the point of view of an audience admiring a successful creation in architecture or music. But now, gazing at the portrait to which he himself is audience, Hopkins is prompted to turn his gaze toward the absent painter's own view: how does the artist himself explain the arrival of inspiration? Hopkins asserts, drawing on Wordsworth, that our inner aesthetic sense—physiological fellow to our other five—is as helpless not to feel joy in responding to perfection of form as the conventional senses are not to see or hear what presents itself to eye or ear. The aesthetic sense, he discovers, is indistinguishable in nature from the other impressionable senses, of which Wordsworth said, in "Expostulation and Reply,"

> "The eye—it cannot choose but see;
> We cannot bid the ear be still;
> Our bodies feel, where'er they be,
> Against, or with our will."

The aesthetic sense produces responses in us strictly comparable to those that we experience as our natural (and spontaneous) biological responses to seeing, hearing, and tasting. The senses are all natural goods, shaded and variegated, of infinite potential, divinely created, knowing no modification by the will:

> For good grows wild and wide,
> Has shades, is nowhere none;

When Hopkins eventually permitted moral questioning to arise in "How all's to one thing wrought!" he could not avoid the unequivocal question of salvation, of the "right" and the "wrong," so different from the aesthetic judgment of "perfect" or "imperfect."

> But right must seek a side
> And choose for chieftain one.

> What makes the man and what
> The man within that makes:
> Ask whom he serves or not
> Serves and what side he takes.

As Jesus warned of ethical choice, "No man can serve two masters" (Matthew 6:24).

This is Hopkins's inventive argument: just as we cannot choose whether we see or hear or taste, so the aesthetic sense, equally of biological origin in the body, is exempt from serving one master or another. The crucial religious question, "Whom do you serve?" does not apply, Hopkins believes, to poetic inspiration, which arrives not as a decision but as an unexpected event that cannot be willed into being. What any masterpiece offers us is a sense of the mind that invented it, but the mind's temporal potential is infinitely diverse, and the artist-as-bee, though creating honey from the flowers all about him, cannot exhaust the meadow's nectar in a single retrieval. The mind, says the poet, is always awaiting the next perfection arriving unheralded from its indescribable "selfless self of self." Of the artist's flowers and honey he securely says,

> His brightest blooms lie there unblown,
> His sweetest nectar hides behind.

Masterpieces are not the weak records of a life that is no more, as the sentimental watercolor will be when the children are dead. On the contrary, Hopkins declares, masterpieces arrive at a quintessence of mind and medium stronger than architecture, sweeter than music, and of a permanence exceeding that of human life.

The blessed potential of poetic invention had seemed ever fresh at the time that Hopkins, released from the ascetic silence of "The Habit of Perfection," exclaimed "How all's to one thing wrought!" But by the time he composes "On the Portrait of Two Beautiful Young People," he can no longer imagine the poem existing in an independent aesthetic space, aspiring to formal perfection; he has come to understand, through his own suffering, Wordsworth's observations in "Tintern Abbey" that a deep distress had humanized his soul, that poetry must absorb and reflect not only nature but also "The still, sad music of humanity." Hopkins's "music of humanity" was only occasionally "still" and "sad"; rather, his physiological intensity—in which every feeling, from the exalted to the bitter, was heightened to acute nervous pitch—led him, in moral terms, to a witnessing aflame with pity and indignation. Although the masterpiece never cedes the aesthetic plane guaranteeing its existence into futurity, it is nonetheless now obliged, when it treats of human life, to take on the weight of moral judgment.

During the Christmas holiday of Hopkins's composing "On the Portrait," he was completing the last revisions of a poem he had been working on for two years, called "Spelt from Sibyl's Leaves." In his youth, delighting in finding symbols in the world of his own mixed nature as priest and poet, he had written in praise of "pied beauty": "Glory be to God for dappled things." But now he was obliged, morally, to separate all the things of the world, both natural and human, into "twó flocks, twó folds—black, white; | right, wrong." To the lover of the dappled world, this last judgment, arising when "earth | her being has unbound, her dapple is at an end" is an agonizing reduction of the inextinguishable fertility of the creative mind. But what Hopkins has come to understand, in contemplating the scattered leaves of his sybilline book, is, at last, his "selfless self of self." He had given it that name so as to connect it to the self while representing it as alien to the same self: it is "most strange," and above all it is voiceless ("most still"). From it came his moments of inspiration (always already "foredrawn to No or Yes"), which seemed to arrive independently only to be quenched by a force outside himself. Inspiration was, he said in a sonnet dedicated to Robert Bridges and written only six weeks before his death, a delight that "Breathes once and, quenchèd faster than it came, / Leaves yet the mind a mother of immortal song." Hopkins had thought of his inspiration as coming from God, a suitably unknowable source, but "Spelt from Sibyl's Leaves" articulates his shocked understanding that inspiration came entirely from his own self, and that its cause was the constant struggle of opposing on the battlefield of the self, under the unfurled banner of the integral being. It was, he now knows, his own suffering that, over time, kindled the later inspiration that generated his "burning witness." "The selfless self of self" was (as we would say) the unconscious mind sequestering his suffering until it could find its necessary formal attributes and emerge as a shaping inspiration.

Having understood that he was alone with himself in a material world of natural causes, the poet, in his apocalyptic sonnet of unrelieved darkness in which no God appears and heaven is populated only by the natural stars, describes his state as that of a man bound on a rack where he is both the torturer and the tortured. His thoughts, like upper and nether millstones, grind pitilessly, their product his wordless "groans," poetry's last expiring utterance, pain without words. He has necessarily become, now that his being has been unbound, the selfless self of self naked, stretching itself on an instrument of torture, a self unprotected, unhoused, beset by abrading contradictions, strung on

> a rack
> Where, selfwrung, selfstrung, sheathe- and shelterless, |
>   thóughts agaínst thoughts ín groans grínd.

It is this pitiless and accurate self-portrait that has replaced the equivocal portrait of the beautiful children.

The Shaper

WHEN I was young, I wondered what the essential ingredient in a successful lyric poem actually was. I had learned that a poem did not have to have meter and rhyme, that a poem could do without the first person, and that no topic was impossible to poetry. But when I was disappointed in a poem I could not say why it was lifeless. What, I wanted to know, gave satisfying poems their life-likeness and intensity?

At twelve I discovered that poems were not necessarily born as they appeared on the page, but often went through many drafts with seemingly unpredictable changes. I perceived, in astonishment, that poems grow and mutate like living things. But I could not determine the reasons behind the poet's revisions, and I spent a good part of my fifteenth year puzzling over drafts of poems by Dylan Thomas, sent to me in microfiche from the University of Buffalo, which held the originals in enthralling number and variety. Already, Hopkins and Thomas had convinced me of the indispensable value of sound, so what I was trying to deduce from the drafts was the reason for revisions in sound as well as in every other layer of a poem, from plot to commas. I found that by imagining myself into the sensibility of the poet holding the pen (and often copying out each successive draft myself), I could ask "myself" why "I" preferred this word to that, this length of line to that, this tone to that. I was unhappy when I could not "figure out" the motive behind a given change, but by the time I had investigated all the Buffalo holdings (there were, as I recall, about thirty drafts of "Fern Hill" alone), I could guess some plausible motives for alterations: "I" was hunting down a more striking metaphor or a more energetic rhythm or a better stanza-form or a firmer point of view. But I still did not see what was directing the whole suite of changes occurring in the multiple evolutionary episodes of the poet's accumulating pages.

I had already memorized (so as to carry them around with me) many standard anthology pieces, but even making them "mine" did not illuminate the sustaining underlying "law" which I was convinced must be governing all the poet's successive micro-revisions. I resorted to conventional ideas of how other verbal things (dialogues, fictions, arguments) were assembled: logic, listing, working toward and away from a climax, having symmetrical parts, but none of these seemed to offer the law for poems in general. Eventually, after some years, I realized that the deepest determining factor was what Coleridge had referred to as his "shaping spirit of Imagination." (I had glided carelessly over the adjective "shaping," registering only "spirit of Imagination.") A mysterious human function, "shaping," lay hidden within every successful poem: it ruled the construction not only of the whole poem but also of its substructures, down to its multiple individual layers—stanzas, sentences, rhythms, tenses, sounds, articles, point of view, punctuation. My own mind lacked this indispensable ability to make magnetic matches across layers, and the lack explained why I was not a poet, in spite of the verses that I had composed between six and twenty-six (when, doing my thesis, I discovered that what I could write was prose).

What was that shaping function, I enviously wondered, and how did it operate? I had found no answer by introspection or by private composition: much as I was moved and delighted by the result of successful "shaping" (a poem that leapt off the page) and much as I was fascinated by its processes, I still could not understand the sureness of aim of a poem's intrinsic growth toward secure life (even life as a fragment). Hopkins, in his last poem, "To R.B.," compared the growth of a poem within the poet to a long pregnancy: the "sire" of the poem, its founding insight, has receded and seems lost but the mothering mind continues her patient work:

> The widow of an insight lost she lives, with aim
> Now known and hand at work now never wrong.

The composing poet knows when an arriving word matches the original insight and finds its aim: the hand at work is "now never wrong." "Never wrong" was what I had sensed in an achieved poem—that an invisible contour of mind and feeling had preexisted the drafts, and to take on life the poem had to match that initiating (and ever-governing) contour. Every revision was another try at a match, an attempt to obey the glimpsed "law" which had to be fulfilled.

I say all this because when a strange new poet appears, it is not so much the "message" of the poetry that I hope to describe as the manner in which the message reaches us. How does the new voice create itself and what elements are implicitly being chosen or rejected as it speaks and we listen? Reviews of new poetry tend to dwell on the biography of the poet or the topical "message" of emotional concern (nowadays often political or ecological) put forward by the poetry. I always want, instead, an answer to my first question: is this poem one of those that will have the strength to survive? Milton hoped that he "might perhaps leave something so written to aftertimes, as they should not willingly let it die." Poems that can interest readers over centuries do not depend on topic or plot: they are more subtle, and more original, than that. In poems that outlast their own generation, the poet has found a voice and a way of thinking that does not sound or feel like anyone else's. Around the living poems lie the heaps of unoriginal verses of patriotism or love or death that have succumbed to the passage of time. (A few of those, erected into national anthems or religious rituals, remain fixed in cultural memory, whatever their lack of imaginative distinction.)

AND SO, thinking of our impulse to praise the strength of a new poet, I was impelled to write here about a young and "difficult" Vietnamese American poet, Ocean Vuong. The glowing reception of his first two books (a "novel" and a volume of poems) did not quote enough for me to be able to judge them independently: public responses in blurbs and reviews alike understandably spent most of their space on Vuong's heartbreaking life after the Vietnam War. At two, he immigrated to the United States with his family and multiracial mother (expelled from Vietnam) after they were sent to a Philippine refugee camp. The family settled in Hartford, Connecticut, but he was by then abandoned by his father, adding to the family's collective desolation. In Hartford, he forgot his first language while being schooled (and bullied) in English; at adolescence, feeling terror on discovering his own homosexuality and his ambiguity as a mixed-race person, he nonetheless concealed his sexual secret, fell in love, and found embarrassed silent joy in his barren days. Then, as his beautiful and tender mother died of breast cancer, he fell into suicidal depression and drug addiction, ending up hospitalized after an anguished nervous breakdown. Through these vicissitudes, he eventually made his way to recovery, at Brooklyn College and New York University, through a rebirth of self in writing.

When Vuong's third book, a volume of poems called *Time Is a Mother* which appeared in 2022, was given to me that Christmas, I could judge for myself. I was soon set back on my heels by poem after poem. Who would think an elegy could consist of nothing after its title except Amazon receipts? These mute pieces of evidence reveal a history of Vuong's mother under the title "Amazon History of a Former Nail Salon Worker." The "poem" covers twenty-one months (two with no receipts at all). The items listed on the receipts vary, but there are recurrent categories: a painkiller, a gift for a child, some female-linked purchase, something aesthetic, something to eat, job materials. The first two "month-receipts" read:

Mar.

Advil (ibuprofen), 4 pack
Sally Hansen Pink Nail Polish, 6 pack
Clorox Bleach, industrial size
Diane hair pins, 4 pack
Seafoam handheld mirror
"I Love New York" T-shirt, white, small

Apr.

Nongshim Ramen Noodle Bowl, 24 pack
Cotton Balls, 100 count
"Thank You For Your Loyalty" cards, 30 count
Toluene POR-15 40404 Solvent, 1 quart

UV LED Nail Lamp
Cuticle Oil, value pack
Clear Acrylic Nail Tips, 500 count

The reader begins, of necessity, to interpret the receipts: "I see, the woman has found a job—a chair in a nail salon—but she has to buy her own supplies. Whatever her pain is, she is buying Advil in multiples. She rarely leaves the Amazon site without ordering something to bring a smile to the face of her young child. They are poor, living on ramen, the cheapest meal to buy, the easiest to make. And she has bought a rust-preventing toxic paint."

The receipts get shorter and the pain gets worse: in December she is buying "Maximum Strength" Advil. And there is nothing at all under "*Jan.*" Has she been hospitalized? By February she needs a walker, and in March she buys a "Chemo-Glam cotton head scarf, sunrise pink." In April a receipt records "'Warrior Mom' Breast Cancer awareness T-shirt, pink and white," and in May a "Mueller 255 Lumbar Support Back Brace." Back in December, she had been preparing for spring, buying "True-Gro Tulip Bulbs, 24 pcs." But when June comes, there is only one item on the receipt:

Jun.

Birthday Card—"Son, We Will Always Be Together,"
  Snoopy design

In July, horrible to imagine, she orders from Amazon her own funeral urn and a large picture frame (for a photo of her to be left to her son?). August: no receipt. By September, her aesthetic desires still alive, she orders

"Easy-Grow Windowsill herb garden." The receipts for October and November anticipate her funeral, as she buys—knowing she will soon die—a new winter coat and warm socks for her son:

Oct.

YourStory Customized Memorial Plaque, 10 × 8 × 4 in
Winter coat, navy blue, x-small

Nov.

Wool socks, grey, 1 pair

As the apparently random purchases aggregate, they begin to tell a story, demanding to be pieced together by the perplexed reader. Each month's list creates a "stanza-with-variations" of this dual tragedy of a broken mother and her shattered son. At the end, the isolated son, wearing his new coat, stands next to his mother's grave, his only possessions a gaunt photo, an ash-filled urn, and a "Customized Memorial Plaque." This is a version of what Thomas Gray called "The short and simple annals of the poor," but instead of the somber stanzas of "Elegy Written in a Country Churchyard," this chronicle is articulated in the enforced clichés of Amazon Americana, from "Snoopy" to the "Eternity Aluminum Urn," the "Perfect Memories picture frame," and the "YourStory Customized Memorial Plaque."

Struck dumb by my compelled participation in this unprecedented format of grief, I thought: who is this writer who can compose an elegy without using a single "poetic" word? Unconsciously, then consciously, the reader absorbs the bitter irony felt by the poet as he must copy these ignoble commercial words—wrenching for him, the reader, and the poem itself—that have become the stinted vehicle to convey his lovely mother's life and death. This starved funeral "poem" stations a single mourner silently creating a single ritual, the transcription of a symbolic Amazon liturgy. Yes, I would not willingly let this poem die, silenced as I was by Vuong's bold "shaping spirit" which invited me, holding discarded Amazon receipts, to intuit the pathos of his mother's story. This was a poem that bore out Stevens's insight that a convincing poem must, by its composed form, "resist the intelligence / Almost successfully."

What, I then wondered, would this poet do in a more traditional kind of lyric? I turned to a title bearing an immemorial Horatian allusion, "Ars Poetica as the Maker." It is Vuong's version of Genesis, exhibiting what is required in the twenty-first century if credible original creation is to occur: in it we hear the voice of a god as he creates a second Adam from the clay of the earth. This is material that has appeared for centuries in literature, in art, in music; what can the young artist's "shaping spirit of Imagination" do to renew such worn and familiar material? Vuong will—shockingly—play god himself. Did Vuong know that the first vernacular play in medieval France dramatized Genesis, beginning with God's instructing Adam that he was formed from clay, and Adam's responding that he already knows that fact?

> "Adam!"
> "Sire?"
> "Fourmé te ai de limo terre."
> "Ben le sai."

Like the medieval creator of *Le Jeu d'Adam,* Vuong removes the story from Genesis's distant third-person unfolding, "In the beginning God created the heaven and the earth." Like any original artist building on an earlier text, Vuong creates in order to critique or repudiate the status quo of that text (therefore the eager and angry banning of books by church and state alike). As the presiding god, Vuong opens his Genesis obscurely in the first person, offering a series of truncated reasons for an action not yet revealed:

Ars Poetica as the Maker

> *And God saw the light and it was good.*
>   —GENESIS 1:4

Because the butterfly's yellow wing
                        flickering in black mud
was a word
          stranded by its language.
Because no one else
                        was coming—& I ran
out of reasons.
                             So I gathered fistfuls
of ash, dark as ink,
                  hammered them
                              into marrow, into
a skull thick
              enough to keep
          the gentle curse
of dreams. Yes, I aimed
                        for mercy—
but came only close

as building a cage
around the heart. Shutters
over the eyes. Yes,
I gave it hands
despite knowing
that to stretch that clay slab
into five blades of light,
I would go
too far. Because I, too,
needed a place
to hold me. So I dipped
my fingers back
into the fire, pried open
the lower face
until the wound widened
into a throat,
until every leaf shook silver
with that god
-awful scream
& I was done.
& it was human.

Allusions abound here, but Vuong makes sure that a missed allusion does not vitiate the poem: the words survive on their own and the poem remains coherent. His Ars Poetica is a correction of Genesis as well as an allusion to it, and it stems, surely, from Vuong's own formative truth—that without suffering, creation would not burst out of muteness into life. As Keats wrote to his brother George, "Do you not see how necessary a World of Pains and troubles is to school an Intelligence and make it a soul?" The original Eden presented no pains and troubles; the God of Genesis did not create Adam with the intention of allowing him agony so that his blank "Intelligence" might acquire what Keats called "identity." Had the God of Genesis wanted to affirm that Keatsian truth, he would have made "Pains and troubles" intrinsic to life in Eden, so that personal identity—and consequently individual art—could arise there.

Vuong's revision of Genesis is (to quote one of Pound's descriptions of poetry) a "dance of the intellect among words." It requires rehearsal here if the reader is to understand its choreography. In the beginning, according to Vuong's history, there was an apocalyptic fire destroying all of god's creatures, so that nothing now presents itself to "the Maker" as available material for creation except the ashes of aftermath (or so Vuong felt, one assumes, after the incineration of Vietnam by a fire invisible now but still boiling beneath the hostile halves of his country). The god of aftermath, seeing the depopulation of earth, tells us, in his own evasive speech, that he has decided to make a new creature more expressive than the beautiful, suffering, but inarticulate butterfly of his earlier effort. An unidentified questioner has asked this god why he decided, after the butterfly, to engage in further creation, and the god's reasons for recommencing—both cogent and idle—initiate the poem:

> Because the butterfly's yellow wing [had no
>   language with which to express its pain];
> Because no one else / was coming [to repopulate
>   the earth];
> & [because] I ran / out of reasons [not to].

Who is the questioner? The answer becomes evident if one recalls the first and second questions in the Christian catechism: "Who made you?" "God made me." "Why did God make you?" The second, tormented Adam needs an answer, but the god's reasons are slippery and inconsistent, exemplified in form by the changing lineation of his speech.

The narrative continues: the god of aftermath, troubled (like earlier, now extinct, mankind) by the paradoxical "gentle curse / of dreams," creates a clay slab from the sooty ashes and creates five senses ("five blades of light") opening up the world to his experimental postapocalyptic creature. He has thereby gone "too far," because it is the senses that enable his creature to sin and suffer. Blake's hammering god is the model for Vuong's own hammering "Maker": interrogating the Tyger, Blake asks what force created him: "What the hammer? what the chain, / In what furnace was thy brain?" Yet the god invented by Vuong impedes the very senses he created. Because he cannot call them "good," he sets himself further tasks, "building a cage / around the heart" and putting "Shutters / over the eyes." Nonetheless, the god affords (for his own self-interested cultural survival) one form of agency to his nascent Adam (who is as yet an "it"): "Yes, / I gave it hands" so it could create, through art, a visible icon of its god: "I, too, / needed a place / to hold me." "So"—and then the purposeful phrases, one by one (advancing in quasi Anglo-Saxon two-step lines that pause halfway to take thought) reach the unforeseeable conclusion of the god's tripled opening "Because."

Without language, his newly made Adam would, like the helpless butterfly's wing, be beautiful but stranded, and so the god must introduce violence in himself to complete (by self-mimesis) the violent creature who will erupt, because of its unbearable suffering, into articulation. Dipping his fingers back into the fiery magma of creation, the god "pried open / the lower face" of the second Adam, wounding it hideously to compel the scalpel-slash to widen "into a throat." Vuong's poem ends in the incarnate scream of the wounded flesh. Vuong allows, however, before the end, an anticipatory and compensatory flashforward into the silver light of poetic speech, when sibylline leaves (borrowed from Virgil, Hopkins, and Eliot) will flutter as the throat utters itself, with tortured sound, into human life. With the awakening of human language, the god ceases to act, and the parallel clauses ("& I was done"; "& it was human") declare the tragedy of divine metamorphosis as a god takes on human incarnation. (The Christian allusion works if you see it, and the poem works even if you don't.)

Vuong's volume, in its title *Time Is a Mother*, declares that he has experienced a new birth after the extinction-by-breakdown of his former existence: the poet's resurrection is accomplished through the discovery, with time and labor, of self-creation in words. The god of the poem, after allowing his sublime power to wax, humiliates it by gashing it into suffering flesh. Returning to the volcanic *ur*-fire to create his creature's face, he must savage it by widening a slash into a throat, enabling the new Adam, no longer an "it," to gain personal identity. The creator-god vanishes into the creature made in his image and likeness as it assumes its new being: "with that god / -awful scream." "& I was done. / & it was human."

After reading these two poems—one located in the banality of Amazon receipts, the other located in the high drama of Vuong's resurrection into shaped articulation after his mute "death" in breakdown—I hardly expected the black humor and flashing street-life of other poems by Vuong:

> This is the best day ever
> I haven't killed a thing since 2006
> ("Snow Theory")

> Scraped the last $8.48
> from the glass jar.
> Your day's worth of tips
>
> at the nail salon. Enough
> for one hit.
> ("Rise & Shine")

> Hey.
>
> I used to be a fag now I'm a checkbox.
> ("Not Even")

Even the most contemporary of these poems pose some of Vuong's riddles: a single line in "Almost Human" offers not a choice among similar things but an "irrational" choice between dissimilar categories: "It was 2006 or 1865 or .327." This could be translated (with some help from Wikipedia on Vuong's birth date—1988—and the meaning of ".327") as:

> I was eighteen when I learned in a history class that the United States had had a Civil War that ended in 1865: I understood then that what we fled in Vietnam was a Civil War too. And when

I turned eighteen, I read with fear that the .357 magnum revolver used by the police was being replaced by the more lethal .327.

In his "novel," *On Earth We're Briefly Gorgeous,* Vuong sometimes had to interrupt his largely autobiographical narrative in order to supply the factual origin and political dimensions of the war that doomed his family to American poverty (mayonnaise sandwiches), illiteracy (Vuong learned to read at eleven), and the harrowing screams of his grandmother's nightmares. He found in poetry a more accurate way than narrative to sustain his fragmented recollections: he could offer, screen by screen, individual shaped moments of memory. The reader remains alert, wondering what life-events could lie under his elliptical sentences:

> It's been a long time since my body.
> Unbearable, I put it down
> on the earth the way my old man
> rolled dice. It's been a long time since
> time.

The hooking of a "cool" syntax to unbearable sentiment is one of the many ways in which Vuong's language calls attention to itself, making itself visible by unsettling the common rules of narrative expression.

Or Vuong's language demands attention by a spectacular unsettling of time. One formidable twelve-page tour de force called "Künstlerroman" ("Story of the Artist's Life") tracks the poet's life backward, present to past, in ever-new variations. Opening in the full modernity of an electronic "now," the poet is unable to forget his traumatic past:

> After walking forever through it all, I make it to the end.
>
> The REWIND button flashes red _ red _ red.
>
> I sit down and push the button. The screen flicks on[.]

We learn later that the poet is recoiling from his approaching book-launch in an expensive hotel, and his reluctance to advance presses him backwards into and through galleries of visual memory, affixing montages of past over present, present over past, while including such contemporary extremes as repellent snatches from a gay sex chat room accompanied by truncated "dick pics" and a reversal—by this survivor of napalm and family deaths—of the collapse of the Twin Towers and the explosion of bodies. It is a tableau of yearning, this reversal:

> Then the gypsum, calcite, plaster, and lead parti-
> cles rise from the pavement in massive billowing
> clouds, and the North Tower reconstructs itself
> and September's clear and blue again, and the
> people float up, arms open, to stand looking out
> of windows in good suits, in good bones.

This impossible pageant of resurrection, as soon as it is envisaged, expunges any lingering belief in a heavenly afterlife.

On the page following the public death of the Towers, a private crisis, also reversed, transmits "the boy's" shock as he sees his mother knocked down by "his father's fist."

The intimate violence creates a trauma as destructive as any public catastrophe:

> I see the boy walk backward into his house, ease his mother down on the kitchen tiles. His father's fist retracts from her nose, whose shape realigns like a fixed glitch. If I slowed it down here, I might mistake the man's knuckles for a caress[.]

As the auteur of his own film, the poet fancies himself able to carry out on the page the corrections of plot that life itself forbids. His will to reverse time extends in a playful moment to the cosmos itself, as "The Hubble telescope swoops the other way" and "Halley's Comet shoots back behind the trees." Yet this astronomical innocence collides immediately, without even a comma's pause, with the sinister return of human experience "as the Humvees roll, again, into Iraq." The absence of any comma tells the reader that the auteur himself cannot retain cosmic "innocence" by a willed suspension of human aggression.

VUONG'S LONG "Künstlerroman" exhibits, and argues for, a form of apparently "spontaneous" lyric composition which denies to the poem any of the usual geometric structures—linear, concentric, spiralling, vortical—that confer architectural coherence. Rather, it favors an "open" field of concern in which many futures offer themselves (a manner that underlies Whitman's expansive catalogues and far-flung geographical surveys). In Vuong's repeated reversals of sequence, the open field reaches us in a distorted way, as if perspective, grid, and climax are all inhibited when one has seen too much too young. It is a nonrealistic realism, undeniable in its specific details but surreal in its irregular procedures, unloosing a successively crushing series of ungovernable effects.

Here and elsewhere in Vuong, the shaping spirit of imagination is the great mover. Routine sequential transcription—too often the fallback form for current American lyric—feels thin and lifeless next to Vuong's passionate lines of symbolic dislocation, where his images become incarnate in disturbingly disordered temporal or spatial form. How did this practice become native to the young poet? He reveals his ecstatic moment of liberation from narrative convention at Brooklyn College, when his teacher Ben Lerner tells him, "You can do anything in poetry." At that permission, the young writer's driving confessional compulsion achieves its fusion with both the surrealism of his fragmented recollections and his corresponding linguistic distortions in grammar, syntax, and hierarchy. A painful linguistic choreography takes place as images confused by childhood perceptions and a frustratingly unwieldable school English coincide with the later confusions of addiction and breakdown provoking aroused despair, all to be enacted in an English betraying its alienated origins and beset by its compensatory furies. The idealistic Western art-fiction of a beautiful feminine Muse inspiring a dreamily reflective composer is put to rout in these poems, where the artist is buffeted by a psychic whirlwind of competing and irreconcilable facts, wishes, dreams, terrors, and regrets. It is a rich dynamic for an undeniable voice, fiercely directed by a shaping imagination as relentless as its raw material.

Artless Art

The Lamb

> Little Lamb who made thee
> Dost thou know who made thee
Gave thee life & bid thee feed.
By the stream & o'er the mead;
Gave thee clothing of delight,
Softest clothing wooly bright;
Gave thee such a tender voice,
Making all the vales rejoice!
> Little Lamb who made thee
> Dost thou know who made thee

> Little Lamb I'll tell thee,
> Little Lamb I'll tell thee!
He is called by thy name,
For he calls himself a Lamb:
He is meek & he is mild,
He became a little child:
I a child & thou a lamb,
We are called by his name.
> Little Lamb God bless thee.
> Little Lamb God bless thee.

WILLIAM BLAKE

NOTHING IS harder to comment on than a piece of art which successfully pretends to artlessness, to be "merely" transcribing what a voice utters—or seems to utter: in real life nobody actually converses in rhyme, but readers of rhymed or rhythmic poetry accept the pentameters of "To be or not to be" as Hamlet's "natural" way of speaking, just as audiences of opera accept the convention that whatever Rodolfo is "saying" to Mimi will be conveyed in song. In the rhyming lines of William Blake's "The Lamb," we hear a single voice speaking, in rhyme; there is no narrator, no editorial comment, no concluding summary. And no self-revelation by the artist-author.

Although Blake was fiercely concerned with politics, and within a few years was to write long poems called *The French Revolution* and *America,* his little illustrated booklet called (and I imitate the original typeface) SONGS *of Innocence*, which appeared in 1789, offered poems of a simplicity that was hailed then (and sometimes even now) as "pure," "childlike," "transparent," "sweet," and of course "innocent." The *Songs* utterly baffled me—as the productions of a grown man—when I first encountered them in high school, and I set them aside in favor of any poem (from Milton's "Nativity Ode" to Keats's "Ode on a Grecian Urn") which seemed properly and deeply reflective in thought and language. (Poems are meant, said Stevens, "to help us live our lives," and in high school that was what I wanted from them.)

Later I decided, before even entering a doctoral program, that I wanted to write a dissertation on W. B. Yeats, but I knew that I had first to understand Blake. Yeats, in his twenties, had co-edited Blake's works, and derived from them aspects of his own theory of poetry. When I entered Harvard's graduate program, seeing that no course was addressing Blake in detail, I asked one of my professors to direct a semester-long "reading course" on Blake for me. Since he generously agreed, we met every week and read all of Blake's poetry. My teacher tolerated our initial pursuit, but when my later papers began to concern Blake's long "prophetic books"—mythological, obscure, and stormy fantasies about weirdly named people ("Oothoon") living in weirdly named places ("Golgonooza")—he groaned and said, "Helen, the *awful* things you are having me read!" But Yeats, following Blake's declaration that "I must Create a System, or be enslav'd by another Mans," indeed developed his own erratic mythological system, called *A Vision*, and my (imperfect) absorption of Blake gave me an entrance to writing on it. (My dissertation on Yeats became my first book, and I am still grateful to that reluctant teacher.)

Blake's long poems, composed, like oratorios, of arias and choruses, are accompanied by his stunning but mysterious illustrations. (They may be found online in *The William Blake Archive*.) They puzzled me, but I was still more puzzled by the ostentatious simplicity of "The Lamb" and other poems in his *Songs of Innocence*. Was there more to this artless art than I could see? I had faith in the sincerity of Blake's promise to his readers in *Jerusalem*, composed between 1804 and 1820:

> I give you the end of a golden string,
>   Only wind it into a ball:
> It will lead you in at Heavens gate,
>   Built in Jerusalems wall.

But how to find the golden string? An unforgettable lyric usually startles by some original feature, some conceptual or linguistic thread calling attention to itself. With intuition and investigation, the clue glows, the golden ball is wound up, and the poem assembles itself into an intelligible structure. But I could not find, for many years, any such golden string of entrance into "The Lamb."

BEFORE INTRODUCING "The Lamb," and explaining my dissent from the usual readings, I must add something about the origin and form of Blake's two lyric sequences, *Songs of Innocence* and *Songs of Experience*. Even before he issued his engraved *Songs of Innocence*—with its appealing title page, elaborately designed, minutely populated, and beautifully colored—Blake had composed, as we know from his notebooks, dark poems, shocked and shocking, centered on female betrayal and male jealousy. In 1794, with *Songs of Innocence* completed, Blake published some of those despairing notebook poems with other lyrics in a collection called (I reproduce the text-format) SONGS *of* Experience, emphasizing the difference from the earlier sequence by repudiating the italic font of *Innocence* in favor of roman for Experience. He released only four copies of this booklet because he had changed his mind about the actual relation of the two sequences to each other. They should not, he realized, be presented as opposites but as complements. That same year, he began publishing the two sequences together, twinned in a single volume which bore an expansive and informative title page, cunningly expressive via the fonts ROMAN and *italic,* changing even the small introductory word "of" in its first two appearances to expose the contrast in the sequences: SONGS of *Innocence and Of Experience, Shewing the Two Contrary States of the Human Soul.* At the foot of the title page lie the prostrate figures of Adam and Eve wearing fig-leaves after their expulsion from Eden.

In spite of Blake's blunt assertion that his poems convey "the two contrary states of the human soul," readers persisted in identifying Innocence with Childhood and Experience with Adulthood, identifying the two "Contrary States" as successive life-periods rather than as fluctuating emotional and intellectual moods. If the two states of the human soul ("the" restricts them to only two) are recurrent from infancy to death, they might more accurately be designated Naïveté and Knowledge. They can in fact be two equally true renditions that allegorize a single event, as in, for example, the paired poems about the birth of a child, "Infant Joy" and "Infant Sorrow." In *Innocence*, under the title "Infant Joy," a young mother imagines a virtual dialogue with her newborn but as yet unbaptized child. "Infant Joy" could more properly be called "A Mother's Joy," since it describes her state of mind. The speechless infant (Latin *infans*, "unable to speak") seems to be requesting that the mother confer on it a pre-baptismal "human" name in lieu of the ecclesiastically required saint's name:

> I have no name
> I am but two days old.—

The mother immediately responds, deferring to the baby's implied wish,

> What shall I call thee?

The infant names itself (or, rather, the mother, once again, imagines what she would like to have the baby say):

> I happy am
> Joy is my name,—

And the mother offers a hopeful prayer for her child:

> Sweet joy befall thee!

The baby's "self-chosen" name, perhaps imagined by the mother (as Leo Damrosch suggests) as the capitalized female name "Joy," is thus made identical with its hoped-for fate (a lowercase "joy") and the elation of reciprocal exchange ("Joy" from the infant, "joy" from the mother) in the (imagined) dialogue begins to be felt.

The baby's original "self-chosen" adjective was "happy," and the mother in the second stanza, where dialogue ceases, provides the second of her own two adjectives (she has already uttered "Sweet," necessarily true of the abstraction "Joy"). Now, gazing at the bodily form of her infant, she chooses "Pretty," an aesthetic characterization, suitably small:

> Pretty joy!
> Sweet joy but two days old.
> Sweet joy I call thee:
> Thou dost smile.
> I sing the while
> Sweet joy befall thee.

The young mother addresses her silent baby in Blakean baby talk, cooing in repetition her "Pretty" and "Sweet," while recording the mutual and simultaneous happiness of mother and child. "Sweet joy I call thee," says the mother, caroling a series of praises in her delusion that she understands what her baby is "saying" and that it understands what she is "saying back." It is actually her own upbrimming joy that the singing mother projects into the "smile" of her infant in this "innocent" ventriloquial, alliterating, and rhyming companionship: "Thou dost smile. / I sing the while."

By his conclusive title-page-twinning of *Innocence* and *Experience* in 1794, and by characterizing the two nouns as "Contrary States," Blake is embodying the law he had announced a year earlier in *The Marriage of Heaven and Hell*: "Without Contraries is no progression." He now asks himself to enlarge his perception by imagining a Contrary to maternal joy, expanding from Joy to Sorrow as he holds contrary moods in his mind at the same moment. While the fond mother is preparing her soul to dote on her child, what must be the state of soul of the actual newborn infant?

"Infant Sorrow," the baleful song of *Experience* corresponding to "Infant Joy," is an enraged monologue from the infant as he (who is ungendered in the poem; I use "he" for convenience) recapitulates the ignominy of his birth. With three paralleled verbs ("groand," "wept" and "leapt") he fuses his tortured and unarmed birth-leap into dangerous Infant-Experience with the simultaneous dismal fall into Parent-Experience of his appalled mother and father. He pipes his birth cry as his mother groans in agony and his father bursts into tears:

> My mother groand! my father wept.
> Into the dangerous world I leapt:
> Helpless, naked, piping loud;
> Like a fiend hid in a cloud.

Who is thinking that the baby, with his unintelligible scream, is arriving like a monstrous "fiend hid in a cloud"? His mother, of course, as we know from Blake's draft of a different poem, "A Little Boy Lost," in which a child—a truth-teller like Lear's Cordelia—says that he cannot love his parents more than himself. Hearing that reasonable assertion, the mother cries out in revulsion, "O that I such a fiend should bear." (That Blake ultimately transfers the word "fiend" to a sadistic priest who burns the baby alive in "a holy place" does not erase, from the mind of the modern reader who knows the draft, Blake's initial impulse to let the demonic epithet emerge from the mother.)

Just as he had "channeled" in "Infant Joy" the young mother's delusion that she and the baby are in dialogue, so, as he continues "Infant Sorrow," Blake "channels" the resentful baby's angry thoughts as he announces the elements of his state, binding them by alliteration—he struggles, strives, and sulks:

> Struggling in my fathers hands:
> Striving against my swadling bands:
> Bound and weary I thought best
> To sulk upon my mothers breast.

Although the infant writhes to escape the constraints of both nature (his father's grip) and culture (the binding swaddling bands), he finds himself helpless, and sinks back, with no "Infant Joy" at all, to sulk upon his mother's breast. And since Joy and Sorrow are two contrary states of the human soul, the allegorized Joy (in a mother) and Sorrow (in an infant) can arrive simultaneously on the poet's page. The mother's idea of the joyous internal state of her baby is pathetically naïve, while the baby's infernal idea of itself—from its first horrible Experience—is entirely credible.

It must not be forgotten, in reading such songs as

"Infant Joy" and "The Lamb," that every single poem in *Songs of Innocence* has been written by an adult being who knows exactly what Experience always brings. The reader's consciousness of the concealed adult author of *Innocence* must figure in any account of Blake's art in the artlessness of "The Lamb." I differ from earlier readers in believing that the poem "The Lamb" is—when we look at its companion poem in *Experience,* "The Tyger"—composed by the author-as-Tyger looking back with pity, on its deluded childhood state. The Tyger, accustomed in his early life to being a docile Lamb, has suddenly awakened in a wholly unfamiliar body, burning with the inner flame and armed with teeth and claws. We must see the nature of the child-speaker through the Tyger's lens, because we too are Experienced (as well as perpetually Innocent), passing constantly, in each episode of life, from Ignorance to Knowledge, from naïveté to awareness. Throughout our life, if we do not refuse perception of our soul-states, we continue to undergo successive falls into Experience. In Blake's long poem *Vala, or the Four Zoas*, one character (speaking, we understand, for Blake himself) sums up the price of the soul's repeated passage from ignorance to awareness, from error to wisdom, from hope to desolation:

> What is the price of Experience do men buy it for
>   a song?
> Or wisdom for a dance in the street? No it is bought
>   with the price
> Of all that a man hath his house his wife his children
> Wisdom is sold in the desolate market where none
>   come to buy
> And in the witherd field where the farmer plows for
>   bread in vain[.]

Wʜᴀᴛ, ᴛʜᴇɴ, are we to make of "The Lamb"? It was sometimes carelessly thought that Blake was speaking in his own voice to the Lamb, but the single line "I a child & thou a Lamb" establishes that Blake has created a fictional child who speaks to an equally fictional Lamb. The two initial questions put to the Lamb by the child seem innocent enough, since they reproduce the first question in the Christian catechism as adapted for children: "Who made you?" (This calls up its answer, "God made me.") Any churchgoing Christian of Blake's day would recognize the child's biblical allusions: from Psalm 23, "He maketh me to lie down in green pastures: he leadeth me beside the still waters"; and from Psalm 114, a metaphor of nature expressing lamb-like joy: "The mountains skipped like rams, and the little hills like lambs." There seems nothing here to "interpret," once one recognizes the Christian references echoed by the churchgoing child-speaker: he knows that God made the Lamb; that John the Baptist called Jesus "the Lamb of God" and that Jesus applied the epithet to himself; that God (as Jesus) became a "little child"; and that Jesus said, "learn of me; for I am meek and lowly in heart." The Christian reader would also know that the child has sung Charles Wesley's two hymns for children (published in 1742): "Gentle Jesus, meek and mild, / Look upon a little child," and "Lamb of God, I look to thee; / Thou shalt my example be; / Thou art gentle, meek and mild; / Thou wast once a little child." It seems that the child is now charmingly conveying his religious knowledge to a "little lamb," met in the meadow. The invisible author of the poem is presumably delighting in his vignette of a young child as innocent "teacher."

The child makes his first departure from religious echo-paraphrase into unconscious originality as his attention turns—with no feeling of impropriety—from received doctrine to his bodily senses of touch and vision. Lambs in the meadow are to him huggable pets, and as he recalls embracing them, he imagines a God who has bestowed on the Lamb his unbiblical "Softest clothing wooly bright." In fact, Blake reproduces the "hug" in *Innocence* via the poem called "Spring," in which the child-speaker converses (in wholly sensuous terms) with a Lamb: the child has not yet been brought under the Vicar's indoctrination.

> Little Lamb
> Here I am,
> Come and lick
> My white neck.
> Let me pull
> Your soft Wool.
> Let me kiss
> Your soft face.

I propose that Blake knowingly composed "The Lamb" as an ironic text. Because the poem has a child-speaker, Blake has decided on stylistic simplicity in its stanza form, rhyming, rhythm, vocabulary, grammar, syntax, and two-stanza structure. Critics have had very little to say, therefore, about "The Lamb," preferring by far to expatiate upon its paired *Experience* poem, "The Tyger."

> Tyger Tyger, burning bright,
> In the forests of the night;
> What immortal hand or eye,
> Could frame thy fearful symmetry?

The speakers of the two poems seem like wholly different personages, and the animals they address could hardly be less alike: the child-speaker of "The Lamb" seems to have fellow-feeling for the Lamb, while the speaker of "The Tyger" is terrified by the predator that has appeared before him. The Creator of the beast is imagined as an immortal and inscrutable artist, using both physical force ("hand") and conceptual design ("eye") to inaugurate an unprecedented visual symmetry, not the familiar symmetry of beauty but one of fright and fear. Since selections in anthologies have reinforced the notion that Blake composed *Innocence* about childhood and *Experience* about adulthood, the "paired poems" of the two sequences are examined for difference rather than for resemblance. Yet one must arrive at some view considering the Lamb and the Tyger as Contrary States rather than Opposite Animals.

An ironic reading of "The Lamb" arises from our scrutinizing the little drama between child and Lamb. Under what circumstances did the child learn the truths that he is teaching the Lamb? We deduce that the child has just begun attending the lessons in Christian belief offered to the youngest children of the Infant Class at Sunday School. On the child's first day, the Vicar has humiliated the newcomer by omitting any kind of welcome such as "Little Child, I greet thee, / Little Child, I greet thee," which would match his closing "professional" dismissal: "Little Lamb God bless thee. / Little Lamb God bless thee." Instead the Vicar situates his little student at a disadvantage by putting to him the first question in the catechism—"Who made thee?"—to which the child, not knowing the answer and feeling ignorant, remains dumb. Refusing to reveal the correct answer, the Vicar once again exhibits the child's vacancy of mind, insisting a second time on the question, this time revealing the child's lack of knowledge: "Dost thou know who made thee[?]" The child hangs his head in embarrassment. Having established the child's inferiority, the Vicar finally, in the second stanza, offers the missing answer. "Little child I'll tell thee," he says, then grandly repeats his intention with "Little child I'll tell thee!," implicitly boasting of his own superior knowledge and demonstrating the child's earlier inadequacy of response.

We find ourselves asking, as we think about the poem, why the child has chosen to address a lamb, but as soon as we raise the question, we realize that every local child who has preceded Blake's child in the Infant Class surely knows the answer to the opening question, so that the only available creature younger and more ignorant than himself is the Lamb. The whole drama now presents itself to us as a role-playing drama arranged by the child, in which he is playing the Vicar and the Lamb is cast as his own first-day self. When he, imitating the Vicar, poses the question in its variant form as a determiner of the child's cognitive capacity—"Dost thou know who made thee[?]"— the Lamb is helplessly silent (as the child himself had been). The Lamb, questioned, is satisfactorily speechless, and now the child, addressing the "ignorant" Lamb, can take on, in the second stanza, the satisfactory (if evil) role of the twice triumphant Vicar: "Little Lamb I'll tell thee, / Little Lamb I'll tell thee!"

The Vicar, as we deduce from the poem's reflection of his Infant Class teaching, has been carefully selecting and sanitizing the portions of Christian belief purveyed to the child. The Vicar's lessons never mention the vengeful God of Isaiah and the Psalms, nor the violent Jesus who drives the money changers from the temple, nor why Jesus calls himself a Lamb (metaphorically anticipating the Passover when he will be slaughtered). In fact, although the child has been told the Christmas story ("He became a little child"), the tragic story of the Passion and Crucifixion remains concealed from him, as does the divine virtue of violence in moral condemnation, defamation, or exclusion.

When a child hurting from a visit to the dentist replays the visit with a younger child, the former victim must become of course the pain-inflicting dentist: the whole point of the role-playing is for the child to reverse the roles, to take on the triumph of the victor and thereby triumph over his past passivity. We become spectators of the child's "innocent" sadism as he humiliates the Lamb (thereby revealing the way in which he was himself humiliated by the Vicar). And our heart sinks at how much the child will ultimately have to learn about the life of Jesus—above all, the harsh tragedy of the Crucifixion. The implicit cruelty of the child, as, unaware of his own ignorance, he complacently and proudly dominates the Lamb, represents his first step into Experience as he (by design) defeats the hapless Lamb, his ideal (because languageless) victim.

Even before composing "The Lamb," Blake understood that there never has been, nor could there ever be, a time of entire and sinless Innocence. In a marginal inscription in the manuscript of *The Four Zoas* (never illustrated, never published in the poet's lifetime) he writes:

Unorganized Innocence, An Impossibility
Innocence dwells with Wisdom but never with Ignorance

THE ANIMAL Blake chose as the contrary to the "innocent" Lamb is the Tyger. And the poem, in its short-form lyric drama, recounts, in my view of it, the frightening passage into Experience as the (male) adolescent undergoes it. The little child, formerly clothed in the soft white garment of the docile Lamb, wakes up overnight to sexual power and aggressive physicality as he discovers himself metamorphosed, with no warning, into a Tyger. He has become a predator whose substance is flame and whose habitation is darkness. Apprehensive questions, as rhythmic as the anvil-strokes of the Maker at the forge, burst out of the adolescent as he becomes the protesting witness of his own overnight transformation—by some unseen and apparently malevolent agent—into an unrecognizable and "evil" creature.

This Beast is the result of a Blakean seventh day of Creation. God has already said, "Let us make man in our image, after our likeness." And since a man was indeed created in the image and likeness of God, according to Genesis, can it be that the Tyger is another image and likeness of the divine? And since God has pronounced his creations good, did He smile in approbation as He contemplated His creature of savage strength, the Tyger? The angelic Stars, seeing the Tyger, regard its creation as a catastrophe, because it reveals that human erotic desire and human lust for aggression must be understood as aspects of God: "Did he smile his work to see? / Did he who made the Lamb make thee?" Later, in his illustrations to the book of Job, Blake gives his definitive answer to the adolescent's frightened speculation. The divine "voice out of the whirlwind" represents himself to Job as the creator of two monsters, Behemoth and Leviathan, praising their nature and their powers. In Blake's engraving, the Behemoth of land and the Leviathan of sea, both magnificently hideous, share a single design: inside a circle, Behemoth stands above on land and Leviathan twists below in the sea. The design bears as its subscribed title God's own words to Job: "Behold now Behemoth, which I made with thee." "Did he who made the Lamb make thee?" Yes, the voice has implied, and he made you, Job, and with you Behemoth and Leviathan, the sacred monsters who are as holy as any other creature. "For every thing that lives is holy, life delights in life; / Because the soul of sweet delight can never be defil'd." With those two lines in his *America*, Blake entered his fundamental creed in 1783, even before he twinned *Innocence* with *Experience*.

The adolescent investigating the burning state of his soul knows, as he frames his questions to the Tyger, that there are two fires in nature: the celestial fire of the sun and the volcanic fire underground. Where did the maker find the molten raw material for the Tyger? "In what distant deeps" (of Hell)—and then he must extend the boundaries of the question to the alternative—"or [celestial] skies"—"Burnt the fire of thine eyes?" He answers his own question by admitting the need to search out the fire by ascent into the air: "On what wings dare he aspire?" The fire lives with God: the human soul would be incomplete without sexuality and aggression, lust and war; otherwise, the soul would find itself permanently arrested in the Contrary state, the naïveté of *Innocence*.

The mild appearance of the Tyger in Blake's engraving accompanying the poem has often been criticized, even mocked. But because this Tyger is an image and likeness of God, we must see him as one of the transfigured predators in "the Peaceable Kingdom" prophesied in Isaiah

11:6–7, in which not only does the Wolf dwell with the Lamb, but the carnivores are transformed into herbivores:

> The wolf also shall dwell with the lamb, and the leopard shall lie down with the kid; and the calf and the young lion and the fatling together; and a little child shall lead them. . . . And the lion shall eat straw like the ox.

Blake had once thought (in "Night" in *Innocence*) that this transformation could take place seamlessly, in a final heavenly phase of the predators' existence: after the predators have massacred the herbivores, the "mild spirits" of the sheep inherit celestial new worlds. The lion, weeping tears of gold, joins them there as the guardian of the sheepfold, who tells the lamb, that he, the lion, newly herbivorous, can follow him in grazing:

> And now beside thee bleating lamb,
> I can lie down and sleep;
> Or think on him who bore thy name,
> Graze after thee and weep.
> For wash'd in lifes river,
> My bright mane for ever,
> Shall shine like the gold,
> As I guard o'er the fold.

In this transcendent state of "Organized Innocence," Innocence is no longer ignorant and Experience is no longer destructive.

But Blake found no relief in castrating the Tyger (or the Lion) into a herbivore cohabiting with the Lamb. Instead, in the apocalyptic *Four Zoas*, he constructed a

Last Judgment in which the roaring Lions regain all their strength. The ninth night has come, the grapes of wrath are being trampled, and the harvest grape-wagons are brought to the winepress by "ramping tygers" and "furious lions":

> Then Luvah stood before the wine press all his
>   fiery sons
> Brought up the loaded Waggons with shoutings
>   ramping tygers play
> In the jingling traces furious lions sound the song
>   of joy
> To the golden wheels circling upon the pavement
>   of heaven & all
> The Villages of Luvah ring[.]

Blake, without dismissing individual sexual emotions, aged into despair over collective evils. He declared Love to be the true religion of Jesus, and preached peace by the forgiveness of sins and the eternal brotherhood of man. He ended his last and longest "prophetic book," the *Jerusalem* of ninety-eight illuminated engravings, in visionary prophecy of a redeemed time. In its grand rhetoric, he has come furthest from the concise art and artlessness of *Innocence* and *Experience*.

Does it make any difference to represent "The Lamb" as a poem constituted by irony instead of by innocence? Yes, if it renders a truer account of Blake's representation of Innocence. If the art concealed by its artlessness enlarges our view of Blake's capacity for moral subtlety, then we may see, among his thousands of vigorous lines, more such subtleties. It is not until we have the two poems before us that we perceive the Lamb's four-beat verse-speech to be technically identical (as trochaic tetrameter rhyming couplets) to that of the Tyger, establishing their indivisible continuity of being. Only in the Vicar's word-for-word repeated formal "staging" opening and closing each stanza of "The Lamb" does the child imitate the Vicar's original words, "Little Child who made thee . . . Little Child God bless thee." (The child merely substitutes "Lamb" for the Vicar's "Child.") Only the lines reproducing the Vicar's "professional" speech are written in three-beat form: this is the Vicar's ungenerous rhetoric. But as soon as we move into the Lamb's hazy recollections of church-instruction, we see that he, by contrast, speaks in four-beat lines, ampler than those of the Vicar. The Lamb's utterances are "smooth," with "sweet" rhythms, even though their metrical signature of successive downbeats is not usually a mild music. The four-beat equally trochaic lines of "The Tyger," with their truculent "anvil-beats," reproduce the "grown-up" form of the Lamb's four-beat mildness. We take no particular notice of the meter as we read, "Gave thee life & bid thee feed. / By the stream & o'er the mead"—but who could fail to notice the distortion of sentence-form and the hammering percussive questions in the heated, equally trochaic, downbeats of "The Tyger"?

> What the hammer? what the chain,
> In what furnace was thy brain?
> What the anvil? what dread grasp,
> Dare its deadly terrors clasp?

Keeping the same meter, Blake "acts out" for us the metamorphosis from placidity to terror as Innocence discovers itself mutating from ignorance into Experience.

The art of the artless tempts every artist: its "vitreous

finish" (Heaney on Yeats) repels explanation of its effect. It can be childish (as in "The Lamb") or unbearable ("Those are pearls that were his eyes"). In music it is idyllic (the shepherd's pipe), in art confounding ("This is not a pipe" accompanying a pipe). It grounds theology ("I am that I am") and establishes morality ("Thou shalt not kill"). It can be the quintessence of sublimity: at the heavenly banquet Herbert's final words are "So I did sit and eat." It can have a deadpan humor: "What do you read, my lord?" "Words, words, words." But it is in tragedy that the art of artlessness reaches its greatest eloquence: Desdemona, dying, when asked, "O, who hath done this deed?" replies, "Nobody; I myself." And the broken Lear, bending over the dead Cordelia, comes to the end of language:

> Thou'lt come no more,
> Never, never, never, never, never.

After an unbearable death, nothing comes to mind but Lear's five-word line.

Forced to a Smile

Epitaph on a Hare

Here lies, whom hound did ne'er pursue
    Nor swifter Grey-hound follow,
Whose foot ne'er tainted morning dew
    Nor ear heard huntsman's hallo',

Old Tiney, surliest of his kind,
    Who, nurs'd with tender care
And to domestic bounds confined,
    Was still a wild Jack-hare.

Though duly from my hand he took
    His pittance ev'ry night,
He did it with a jealous look,
    And, when he could, would bite.

His diet was of wheaten bread
    And milk, and oats, and straw,
Thistles, or lettuces instead,
    With sand to scour his maw.

On twigs of hawthorn he regaled,
    On pippins' russet peel,
And, when his juicey sallads fail'd,
    Sliced carrot pleased him well.

A Turkey carpet was his lawn
    Whereon he lov'd to bound,
To skip and gambol like a fawn,
    And swing his rump around.

His frisking was at evening hours,
  For then he lost his fear,
But most before approaching show'rs
  Or when a storm drew near.

Eight years and five round rolling moons
  He thus saw steal away,
Dozing out all his idle noons,
  And ev'ry night at play.

I kept him for his humour' sake,
  For he would oft beguile
My heart of thoughts that made it ache,
  And force me to a smile.

But now, beneath this walnut-shade
  He finds his long last home,
And waits in snug concealment laid
  'Till gentler Puss shall come.

He, still more aged, feels the shocks
  From which no care can save,
And, part'ner once of Tiney's Box,
  Must soon partake his grave.

WILLIAM COWPER

A N EPITAPH—the short inscription on a tombstone—
normally names and praises admirable qualities of
the person buried there, and then hopes for a benevolent
future after death. The gravestone may speak to the viewer
in the dead person's voice (as Coleridge imitates the Latin
Siste, viator: "Stop, Christian passer-by—Stop, child of

God . . . O, lift one thought in prayer for S. T. C."), or it may speak as a mourner addressing the buried person (as in the Latin, *Sit tibi terra levis,* "May the earth lie light upon you"). In his "An Essay on Epitaphs," written a few years after William Cowper's birth, Dr. Johnson restricts epitaphs to "heroes and wise men" deserving of praise: "we find no people acquainted with the use of letters, that omitted to grace the tombs of their heroes and wise men with panegyrical inscriptions." The readers of "Epitaph on a Hare" by William Cowper (pronounced "Cooper") would have expected just those qualities in any epitaph: it would celebrate a male either wise or heroic, and its praise would be public and formal. (The Greek roots of "panegyric" mean "an assembly of all the people.")

Against such prescriptive forms, the only obligation for an ambitious poet writing an epitaph is to be original. The form becomes memorable by dispensing with or altering conventional moves: Yeats brusquely repudiates Coleridge's "Stop, Christian passer-by," in his own succinct self-epitaph: "Cast a cold eye / On life, on death. / Horseman, pass by!" Keats, dying in his twenties, refused the first, indispensable element of an epitaph, a name, and wanted only "Here lies One Whose Name was writ in Water."

As soon as animals became domestic pets, they could become the subject of an epitaph; Byron wrote a long epitaph on his dog, and had it inscribed on a large tombstone. (On the grounds of at least one of the colleges at Cambridge, there is a cemetery for pets of the dons which includes inscribed tombstones and small sculpted monuments.) Nowadays, in a practice that would have scandalized the pious of past eras, newspaper death notices in the United States commonly include, among the named survivors, domestic pets. The subject of Cowper's epitaph is not domesticated, but wild—"a wild Jack-hare"—not a hero, not a human being, hardly even a pet, but one nonetheless named and distinguished from its fellow hares.

The most original epitaph for a pet in English literature, Cowper's "Epitaph on a Hare" is a poem utterly dependent on charm. Poets writing on death have traditionally preferred to create either a somber "philosophical" meditation (on time, regret, the afterlife, and so on) or a direct expression of personal grief. By contrast, charm in lyric requires a complex management of tone: it cannot be single-mindedly earnest or single-mindedly sorrowful, nor can it be unconscious of its hearers. It is a social utterance. It needs a stylized attitude of wistfulness and irony, a blending of the impersonal with the personal, of the independent mind with the troubled heart, and above all, it requires an evident awareness of itself and its listeners.

In real life, charm is almost as rare as exceptional beauty: beauty is Fate's gift, but charm is a quality of personality and behavior. And charm is always remarked with a lightness of tone; it concerns something small, not sublime or heroic. The praise of charm is always tinged with pathos, charm being such a transient quality. Yeats, reflecting in "Memory" on the women he had loved (if imperfectly) over a long life, comments on the relative rarity of loveliness and charm among those women: "One had a lovely face / And two or three had charm." But neither loveliness nor charm could transfix him for life, as had the wild beauty of Maud Gonne's presence:

> One had a lovely face,
> And two or three had charm,

> But charm and face were in vain
> Because the mountain grass
> Cannot but keep the form
> Where the mountain hare has lain.

That his love for Gonne was a quality of the flesh is stipulated by Yeats's finishing this little poem with an unignorable match of the botanical and the animal: the *mountain* grass cannot forget the "form" (the image impressed on it) by the couched *mountain* hare. Grass-bed and hare belong to each other not because of any human kinship of "mind" or "soul," but because (Yeats's repeated noun tells us) both are denizens of the mountain, grass and flesh born of the same territory.

Yeats chooses a formal rhyme scheme for his poem on unforgettable beauty, but his slightly unsettling scheme does not employ the familiar couplet or quatrain; instead, it is a freestanding sestet, *abcabc*. And its slant rhymes are at first uncertain: does "grass" indeed rhyme with "face"? Will "form" eventually rhyme with "charm"? Only at the sixth line, where "lain" emphatically rhymes with "vain," is the scheme fully intelligible. So unprecedented, so confusing, is heroic beauty that an unsettled air must hover over the lines until the conclusive arrival at "lain."

In Yeats's "Memory," charm is somewhat bewildering, a possession of only "two or three" in an erotic lifetime; it comes etymologically from the Latin *carmen*, "song," and is related to "incantation." It has magic power, it lays a spell, it is alluring, it overcomes resistance, it "pleases greatly" (according to my dictionary). On the other hand, unlike striking beauty, charm has to be ascribed to something relatively approachable, of a domestic size, like the "charm" on a "charm bracelet." It never claims too much; it can never be theatrical. And something about it is odd, as Robert Herrick knew: it is odd to be sexually "bewitched" by something which is rationally offputting (distracting, neglectful, careless) but psychically fascinating, since it intimates a "wantonness" within:

> A sweet disorder in the dress
> Kindles in clothes a wantonness;
> A lawn about the shoulders thrown
> Into a fine distraction;
> An erring lace, which here and there
> Enthrals the crimson stomacher;
> A cuff neglectful, and thereby
> Ribands to flow confusedly;
> A winning wave, deserving note,
> In the tempestuous petticoat;
> A careless shoe-string, in whose tie
> I see a wild civility:
> Do more bewitch me, than when art
> Is too precise in every part.

Our contemporary master of charm in verse was James Merrill, who, at forty-three, dared to close his eight-sonnet sequence on opera, "Matinées," with a version of the "naïve" note of thanks (made into halting verse) that he had sent, at the age of twelve, to his mother's friend who had invited him to join her at the Metropolitan Opera for *Das Rheingold*. Miraculously, the note has mutated into a childishly "awkward" sonnet (following on seven sonnets of symphonic eloquence):

> Dear Mrs. Livingston,
> I want to say that I am still in a daze

From yesterday afternoon.
I will treasure the experience always—

My very first Grand Opera! It was very
Thoughtful of you to invite
Me and am so sorry
That I was late, and for my coughing fit.

I play my record of the Overture
Over and over. I pretend
I am still sitting in the theater.

I also wrote a poem which my Mother
Says I should copy out and send.
Ever gratefully, Your little friend . . .

The "little friend" is still shaky on prosody, while proud of his rhymes. And by replicating, mistakes and all, the perfect rapture he expressed at twelve, Merrill demonstrates with witty charm that he is as susceptible now as then to the effect of the rising of the curtain on the music of the Rhine maidens, "No one believing, everybody thrilled." The charm also lies in his decision to let his youthful mistake stand: *Das Rheingold* has a Prelude but no "Overture."

Some usual elements of poetic "charm" in lyric, then, are a slightly perplexing initial effect, unconventional elements (of topic, of addressee), a wayward use of genre, ironic sidelights, and a playful spirit. They all meet in William Cowper's surprising epitaph-poem.

SEEING AN elegiac commemoration of "a wild Jack-hare," we wonder how such an epitaph came to be composed, and why it is so moving. Its success arises from the double self-awareness of the poet; he is fully conscious of his own actual grief and equally conscious of the unconventional and comic way in which he is speaking. Above all, he expects his readers to follow his own amusement at the mixed language that he must invent for such an unlikely subject without losing sight of what exigencies call forth its parodic features.

William Cowper, who was born in 1731 and died in 1800, was an English clergyman and the son of a clergyman. After a beatific episode in which he felt close to, and loved by, God, he fell into a lifelong despairing conviction that he was predestined to be damned, eternally unredeemable. He was hospitalized for months after a suicide attempt, and was unable in life to function as a clergyman. Retreating from the practice of his profession, but with a small inheritance, he took up residence with Morley Unwin, a clergyman friend, and his wife and child; and when the clergyman died, he continued to live with the compassionate wife, Mary Unwin, who devoted herself to him and was his chief human comfort during his recurrent periods of insanity.

Over time, in his saner periods, Cowper became the author of many essayistic pentameter poems that range from peaceful descriptions of pastoral life to outspoken denunciations of colonial slavery. But he also wrote trenchant introspective lyrics, of which the most famous is "The Cast-Away," a "posthumous" past-tense description of his own death, comparing it to the fate of a sailor who fell overboard and could not be saved. Recalling Jesus's calming of the waves of Galilee with "Peace, be still," Cowper says bitterly that he and the doomed sailor had no such resource, none:

No voice divine the storm allay'd,
    No light propitious shone,
When, snatch'd from all effectual aid,
    We perish'd, each, alone;
But I, beneath a rougher sea,
And whelm'd in deeper gulphs than he.

The devastating effect of "We perish'd, each, alone" is outdone by Cowper's two-line tragic footnote, a trapdoor to a worse hell than the sailor's: a "rougher" and "deeper" fate lies in religious despair than in bodily death.

Cowper's mother died at his birth, and five of his siblings also died. As an adult—unmarried, childless, profoundly melancholy, suicidal, on several occasions wretchedly confined for insanity—Cowper must have been one of the loneliest poets of our language. Isolated at the house in Olney that he shared in his adult life with Mary Unwin, he built wooden cages in which he kept as pets first a single hare, which he received as a gift, but eventually three wild male hares. They spent the day in the garden, and at evening Cowper would admit them to the parlor, tenderly watching them play together in his presence. He wrote an essay-letter for *The Gentleman's Magazine* describing them—"Puss, Tiney, and Bess" (all males)—and revealing, though reticently, the extent to which they benefited him during his anguished depressions. He perceived, he confessed, "that in the management of such an animal, and in the attempt to tame it, I should find just that sort of employment which my case required."

Cowper nursed his hares when they were ill, carried them about in his arms, and dutifully took to obeying their wishes, studying their disparate temperaments. Puss, as he explained to readers of his magazine piece, was grateful to him for the care he showed, but "Not so Tiney. . . . if, after his recovery I took the liberty to stroke him, he would grunt, strike with his fore feet, spring forward and bite. He was, however, very entertaining in his way, even his surliness was matter of mirth." Bess was "a hare of great humour and drollery," and became tame "from the beginning." Cowper's letter describes dispassionately the hares' diet and their seasonal preferences ("during the winter, when vegetables are not to be got, I mingled their mess [i.e., meal] of bread with shreds of carrot," and so on). Throughout the essay, Cowper endeavors to persuade his reader that hares are the most appealing of animals: the "sportsman," hunting not for food but merely to kill, "little knows what amiable creatures he persecutes, of what gratitude they are capable, how cheerful they are in their spirits, what enjoyment they have of life."

Besides this reminiscent essay and his "Epitaph on a Hare," Cowper added, to keep Tiney alive in memory, a Latin epitaph: "Epitaphium Alterum" ("Another Epitaph"). Like the English poem, it begins with the conventional *Hic jacet,* "Here lies," and repeats the conventional address to the passerby, but it still divagates from the classic human epitaph in celebrating Tiney's lucky life, sheltered by his owner from both human predators and the unkindness of nature: "No huntsman's bound, / No leaden ball, / No snare, / No drenching downpour, / Brought about his end." The epitaph closes unconventionally, too, as the mourner unexpectedly assimilates his own death to Tiney's: "yet he is dead— / And I too shall die": "Tamen mortuus est— / Et moriar ego."

So, flanking the verse "Epitaph on a Hare," we find the detailed gentlemanly letter and the Latin epitaph, each more public than the poem; and it is against such relatively impersonal documents that the "Epitaph on a Hare" shines in its humor and its sadness. Almost every stanza contains a surprise. In the first, we are introduced to the mysteriously protected life of an unnamed wild, not domestic, animal; in the second, we encounter the initially withheld pet-name (which "should" have immediately followed the "Here lies") and also the reversal of the usual superlatives (not "noblest" but "surliest"); in the third, the mounting list of the hare's doings, climaxing not with a heroic or saintly action but rather with the doubly stressed comic end-words, "would bite." The mourner has been obscured, too; his relation to the hare is given only meagerly in the third stanza, with the unrevealing phrase "my hand."

These strange and deviant beginnings are, as I say, surprising in themselves, but the great triumph of the poem comes in its next four stanzas, the ones on Tiney's diet and behavior. It takes a bit of time for us to understand that Cowper is parodying the doting diction of a young mother, who assumes, in her maternal fondness, that her interlocutor-bystander is as interested as she in her baby's important dietary preferences and daily amusements. Translated to our contemporary moment, the young mother would be earnestly explaining her endeavors to feed her baby the choicest of items and expressing her chagrin when a store has run out of a favored ingredient: "Jimmy really adores the Gerber mixed berries, but there wasn't a single jar on the shelf, and I was worried, but I did find the cereal and the applesauce that he usually has for breakfast, and some favorite vegetables—puréed peas and squash. And then I found a new mix, too, with chicken in it, that he was willing to try when I gave it to him for dinner." The bystander hopes that this is the end of the recital, but no, now it is her Jimmy's behavior—how much he clings to his stuffed animals, especially the pet elephant, and how vigorously he pedals in his little swing. Nor does she stop there, but advances to her baby's preferred time of day and his response to a change in the weather: "You know, when everything settles down after dinner, he's much more playful, and then, when a storm is coming, he senses it and gets really excited." By this time the bystander is backing away.

Cowper parodies the dilated intimacy of the mother's discourse with much amusement, listening to himself. The interminable list of foods, and the owner's anxiety if something cannot be found, spill out on the page in an excessive inventory of ten items. Difficulties yield to happy solutions as Cowper continues to imitate "maternal" anxiety ("and then, if I lacked thistles, I'd find lettuce for him"). We are made to feel the wild hare's joy as he "regales" on his special provender. (The *Oxford English Dictionary* cites John Adams in 1771, resolving to make a pool with clear water, so that "the Cattle, and Hogs, and Ducks may regale themselves here.") As the named foods become more adjectivally specific—"twigs of hawthorn," "pippins' russet peel," "juicey sallads," "Sliced carrot"—the owner's extravagant affection mounts. The list ends with the unconcealed triumph of the owner over seasonal scarcity, as he succeeds in substituting alternate foods for scarce ones. Has there ever been a more absurd climax than the proud victory of Tiney's owner announcing that "when his juicey sallads fail'd, / Sliced carrot pleased him well"? And has there ever been a public epitaph that listed the epicurean delights of a lovingly chosen cuisine for an ungainly pet?

Cowper is a past master of tone and detail. Not only can we hear the tone in which each detail is given, we are even prompted to intuit tones that must have preceded the present ones. We can infer the owner's anticipatory devotion in slicing up all those carrots, reflecting how pleased Tiney will be as he approaches his dish. And Cowper is also a master of diction, knowing just how to join Tiney in his "gambols" by releasing a coarser language: Tiney "lov'd to . . . swing his rump around." The anatomical phrase brings a farmer's speech hovering into view.

The owner of the hares mimics his own worry about Tiney's aging by slipping directly into Tiney's very mind, imagining him counting down his years and months of self-indulgent life:

> Eight years and five round rolling moons
>   He thus saw steal away,
> Dozing out all his idle noons,
>   And ev'ry night at play.

The poet's worry was warranted; Tiney died at nine. And here Cowper at last reveals why Tiney is allowed into his house. It is the poet's first-person confession that makes the whole poem grow in stature and grace:

> I kept him for his humour' sake,
>   For he would oft beguile
> My heart of thoughts that made it ache,
>   And force me to a smile.

The anxious diet-procurement, the seasonal schedule of feeding, the protection from predators, the nightly play—these indeed "beguiled" the poet, as they beguile the epitaph itself, until aching thoughts and a forced smile expose the death's head of the poet's suffering being. Between the separated words "heart" and "ache" lie the terrible fears and the hopelessness in which the poet lives. Those two monosyllabic lines—like the fatal "deeper" and "rougher" comparatives of "The Cast-Away"—intensify the atmosphere to an acute register of pain. That intensity then casts a piercing backlight on the whole epitaph: back over the startling characteristics in "surliest" and "would bite"; over the foolish fondness of "juicey sallads" and "Sliced carrot"; over the aesthetic appreciation of the contrast between the hare's skips and gambols and the heartier pleasure when he would "swing his rump around"; and over the poet's "beguiled" observation of the hare's vicissitudes of response to the weather. The watching, the devotion, the feeding, the cherishing—all the instances of care—are then decoded, with hindsight from the reader, as daily evidence of the aching thoughts and the rare smiles. The unsettling strobe-effect (charm/sorrow, beguilement/ache, play/loneliness) persists in every rereading. The flicker between comedy and heartache is the chief resource of Cowper's charm.

But there are many others: the genuineness of Cowper's loss flickers between the solemn epitaphic frame (from "Here lies" to the ecclesiastical "long, last home") and his elation at Tiney's animal liveliness, between "Here lies" and "would bite." We are charmed not only by the proprietorial boast of the opening: that Tiney was successfully spared, by his assiduous owner, the ritual danger of the morning hunt, but also by the closing view of the hare's affection for his two precariously remaining companions. Finally, we are touched by the way Cowper's past-tense narrative presses forward to amalgamate itself into the "now" and the "this" of the imminent moment of parting. We are made to feel the gap between the poet's relish in his pets and the implication (explicit in the alternate Latin epitaph) of the poet's own death in the closing word, "grave."

Cowper's means are simple: he offers a monosyllabic poem composed largely of monosyllabic lines cast into the familiar form of the ballad stanza, with rarely disturbed iambic rhythms. And it all appears to lead to a "Christian" pathos as Tiney "in snug concealment laid" consciously "waits" for "Puss" to keep him company in the grave. Yet once again, as in "The Cast-Away," Cowper adjusts the end of the poem to a darker note: Puss feels his irrevocable destiny in "the shocks / From which no care can save" and knows he will eventually "partake" (take up space) in Tiney's grave. All communication then ends—between owner and hares, and among the hares themselves, as a long silence—of the shocks, of the grave—ends the poem.

Lest charm and humor wane in a poem so mixing the two with mourning, the harsher edges of life and expression must be framed in a "softer" vision, through which nonetheless—if the poem is to ring true—the death's head must be glimpsed. Others have elegized their pets with playful fondness and appreciation, those natural emotions on losing a companion, but Cowper's many sophisticated and whimsical tones and tableaux of mourning—for himself as well as Tiney—make his epitaph a deeper commemoration.

Is CHARM still exerted in poetry? I have found it recently not only in Merrill but also in A. R. Ammons's no-holds-barred final book, unceremoniously titled *Bosh and Flap-doodle*. The poems, written in old age and illness, combine self-mockery and a *basso continuo* of fear. Ammons calls them "prosetry." At first I didn't know what to make of some of them, their slangy and farcical impudence routing Ammons's general inclination to serious poetry of science and nature. The charm of these "last words" is, as usual, bewildering to the reader. Incomprehensibly and grandly, one poem flaunts the title "America," even though its titular scene—the entire country—seems attached to the minor geriatric problem of dieting. Eventually, the second part of the poem enables another view: America is both personal—when you are chastised into dieting—*and* grand in landscape and weather when you delete personal annoyances in favor of casting your glance more widely. At the close of the poem, which I omit here, the charm lies in the weird separability, and ultimate twinning, of the two points of view: individual and cosmic.

The aging Ammons (in the implied narrative of the first part) has chronically bad dietary habits, and his doctor, wanting him to reform, sends him to a dietician. The poem opens on the poet's "counseling" session with the dietician. Ammons chooses to charm us here by jolting us from voice to voice: one is the voice of the severe dietician, recommending unattractive diet items (and reproving disobedient choices); the second is the voice of the adult poet satirically rephrasing the unwelcome advice; and the third is the undersong of the resentful *sotto voce* id of the patient, who defensively luxuriates in asides as he solicits the memory of appetizing items of past meals, and slips in, at the end of the diet-poem, a resolve to transgress with "an occasional / piece of chocolate-chocolate cake." I have sorted out the voices here, but imagine what it feels like to read "America" fresh off the page, realizing that the title means, for part one, that everyone in the country is endlessly attempting counseling and self-discipline in eating, and endlessly falling back into appetite:

> Eat anything: but hardly any: calories are
> calories: olive oil, chocolate, nuts, raisins
>
> —but don't be deceived about carbohydrates
> and fruits: eat enough and they will make you
>
> as slick as butter (or really excellent cheese,
> say, parmesan, how delightful): but you may
>
> eat as much of nothing as you please, believe
> me: iceberg lettuce, celery stalks, sugarless
>
> bran (watch carrots, they quickly turn to
> sugar): you cannot get away with anything:
>
> eat it and it is in you: so don't eat it: &
> don't think you can eat it and wear it off
>
> running or climbing: refuse the peanut butter
> and sunflower butter and you can sit on your
>
> butt all day and lose weight: down a few
> ounccs of heavyweight ice cream and
>
> sweat your balls (if pertaining) off for hrs
> to no, I say, no avail: so, eat lots of
>
> nothing but little of anything: an occasional
> piece of chocolate-chocolate cake will be all
>
> right, why worry[.]

The serve-and-return pattern of contradictory voicing parodies the counseling session by allowing the things the patient cannot in fact say aloud to rise to the surface. We hear not only his irritation at the attempted control by the dietician, but also his wistful glances back to the delights of parmesan cheese. The smallness of the occasion, the pathos of the geriatric plight, the defiant humor, the fluctuations of tone, the awareness of a reader of unknown gender—"sweat your balls (if pertaining) off"—the witty play with email brevity ("hrs") are all characteristic of charm, in Ammons as in Merrill and Cowper. Trifling with genre always delights the poet: whether Cowper is upending the epitaph, or Merrill is inventing a child's thank-you sonnet, or Ammons is parodying patronizing advice, the poet's self-awareness together with his awareness of an audience makes for a gaily sympathetic and sophisticated performance.

But why is the title of the poem "America"? The first answer, the comic one, the poet would say, is because this is what all America (myself included) is doing—dieting while resenting dieting. But the second answer, the sublime one, arises from the last seven lines of "America," as the declining poet finds when he turns his gaze from the indignities of age to the grandeur of the American landscape. In the landscape he finds an impersonal reassurance in "disaster renewal," the cosmic self-repair of the natural seasons. Satiric "charm" falls away, replaced by awe at the natural resurrections of spring.

"America," with its two contrasting parts, shows that the spell of charm need not be maintained throughout a poem. But the advantage of lyric charm is its capacity to relieve the unreality of an unmixed high seriousness. Instead, one sees oneself as an unimportant speck in an indifferent, if exciting, universe, finding a point of self-regard more independent than earnestness, one not omitting comic truth. Ammons is unsparing on the fact of cosmic indifference; Merrill demonstrates how a more ironic vision has replaced, in adulthood, the naïve sweetness of childhood; and Cowper, like our later poets, does not obscure either the ravages of time or the power of sympathy. Cowper ranges through so many tones and tableaux while mourning his beloved hares that the poem seems not a pet-elegy, but rather a human one. As we follow its exquisite variations on charm and grief, classical reminiscence and personal hardship, we are instructed how three improbable pets, more than two centuries ago, could force a despairing poet to a smile.

The Red Business:
PTSD and the Poet

The Artilleryman's Vision

While my wife at my side lies slumbering, and the wars
   are over long,
And my head on the pillow rests at home, and the vacant
   midnight passes,
And through the stillness, through the dark, I hear, just
   hear, the breath of my infant,
There in the room as I wake from sleep this vision presses
   upon me;
The engagement opens there and then in fantasy unreal,
The skirmishers begin, they crawl cautiously ahead,
   I hear the irregular snap! snap!
I hear the sounds of the different missiles, the short *t-h-t!*
   t-h-t! of the rifle-balls,
I see the shells exploding leaving small white clouds,
   I hear the great shells shrieking as they pass,
The grape like the hum and whirr of wind through the
   trees, (tumultuous now the contest rages,)
All the scenes at the batteries rise in detail before me
   again,
The crashing and smoking, the pride of the men in their
   pieces,
The chief-gunner ranges and sights his piece and selects
   a fuse of the right time,
After firing I see him lean aside and look eagerly off to
   note the effect;
Elsewhere I hear the cry of a regiment charging, (the
   young colonel leads himself this time with brandish'd
   sword,)

I see the gaps cut by the enemy's volleys, (quickly fill'd
up, no delay,)
I breathe the suffocating smoke, then the flat clouds
hover low concealing all;
Now a strange lull for a few seconds, not a shot fired on
either side,
Then resumed the chaos louder than ever, with eager
calls and orders of officers,
While from some distant part of the field the wind wafts
to my ears a shout of applause, (some special success,)
And ever the sound of the cannon far or near, (rousing
even in dreams a devilish exultation and all the old
mad joy in the depths of my soul,)
And ever the hastening of infantry shifting positions,
batteries, cavalry, moving hither and thither,
(The falling, dying, I heed not, the wounded dripping
and red I heed not, some to the rear are hobbling,)
Grime, heat, rush, aide-de-camps galloping by or on a
full run,
With the patter of small arms, the warning *s-s-t* of the
rifles, (these in my vision I hear or see,)
And bombs bursting in air, and at night the vari-color'd
rockets.

WALT WHITMAN

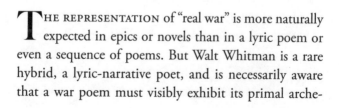

THE REPRESENTATION of "real war" is more naturally
expected in epics or novels than in a lyric poem or
even a sequence of poems. But Walt Whitman is a rare
hybrid, a lyric-narrative poet, and is necessarily aware
that a war poem must visibly exhibit its primal arche-

type in realistic battle. His war poems can be read as a series urgently entering the war through different portals, each attempting to fill a different gap in the imagined panorama, each therefore reflecting the assumed partial inadequacy of the others, and the need for more. To read *Drum-Taps*, his collection of 1865, is to recognize how quickly Whitman realized the banality of his early jingoistic battle-cries and flag-wavings, not to speak of the suppression, in those early war poems, of what he called, with deadly accuracy, "the red business." In 1861, when the Civil War began, Whitman was a man in his forties, a non-combatant who had never himself even been wounded. His most natural lyric genre was a poem spoken in the first person. Could he, should he, ethically assume the voice of an active soldier? Nor was he sure of the stance that he should take toward weapons and their wielders. Was he obliged to portray actual killing? He found comparably troubling questions everywhere in the composition of his war poetry.

In addition to such moral questions, formal questions came thronging, arising inevitably in the perplexities of representing battle. At what point should the poem enter the battle, and how much had the poem to accomplish before it could find an ending? What kind of battle should it present, in what large or small setting? Should it be seen in close-up or from a distance? Who will populate the battle, with what weapons, and in what choreography? How specific must the poem be: should the armies be named, should the cause of the war be articulated? What decorum should a war poem observe: should dead bodies be exposed to view? In a personal lyric such perplexities are more easily solved by ear, eye, and instinct, but when the topic arises from a contemporary war, known in its historical circumstances (from newspapers and military bulletins), how shall the poet enter his nation's current history? And how are his claims to be authenticated? Such questions would arise interiorly in anyone writing a group of war poems.

Whitman made the most active claim to the authenticity of his reportage in the first poem of *Leaves of Grass:* "I am the man, I suffer'd, I was there." Those words bring to a close an anecdote in which the poet learns of the actions of a heroic sea-captain: how he risked following a sinking ship through three stormy days, and how, when the storm abated, the brave captain rescued the traumatized passengers from what would have been their sure death:

> How he saved the drifting company at last,
> How the lank loose-gown'd women look'd when
>   boated from the side of their prepared graves,
> How the silent old-faced infants and the lifted sick,
>   and the sharp-lipp'd unshaved men;

—but at that very moment, within the very same sentence, the narrated story of the captain's acts begins to move, with almost biological caution, step by step, into first-person speech. The poet gradually feels himself mutating into one of the rescued passengers:

> All this I swallow, it tastes good, I like it well,
>   it becomes mine,
> I am the man, I suffer'd, I was there.

His new identity, which at first appears (quite peculiarly) as a present-tense testing of sense-experience—of ingestion, of swallowing, of tasting—comes to life as a complete present-tense being ("I am the man"). The poet then recapitulates the process in the past tense: the poet insists that he is the same man as he was before the assumption of his added identity—that of one saved from death: "I am the man, I suffer'd, I was there." The three "I"s, present and past, fuse into a new immaterial oneness.

Are you the man? Did you suffer? Were you there? How can the reader be persuaded of this extraordinary declaration? And if this is the poet's suffering during a purely "natural" catastrophe—a storm—can he expect the reader to believe him when he takes on the hideous suffering— caused by arbitrary human evil—of "the hounded slave"?

> I am the hounded slave, I wince at the bite of the
>   dogs,
> Hell and despair are upon me, crack and again crack
>   the marksmen,
> I clutch the rails of the fence, my gore dribs, thinn'd
>   with the ooze of my skin,
> I fall on the weeds and stones[.]

Whitman, often pondering the empathetic possibility of union, implicitly authenticated his claim by the accuracy of his vocabulary—his imagination alone was responsible for his convincing portrayal of the population awaiting rescue: the women of the shipwreck, their "lank loose-gown'd" selves, and the sad infants, surprisingly "silent" and "old-faced," the sick needing to be "lifted," the "unshaved men" with their three days' beards. We can even see what the drifting doomed are thinking as they fear "their *prepared* graves."

In a postwar poem, "Sparkles from the Wheel," Whitman clarifies this imagined participatory process, naming it "effusion." As the poet-speaker casually notices a knife-grinder in the street, his impersonal first glance narrows to a directed focus. The focusing awakens in the eager eye an arterial imagination, re-creating the material presence of the poet's physical body as an invisible immaterial one:

> Myself effusing and fluid, a phantom curiously
>   floating, now here absorb'd and arrested[.]

Absorbing, he is absorbed; arrested by the scene, he is arrested into it. Only after his casual physical eyesight fixes on the individual detail of the knife-grinder does his spirit effuse itself (Latin: "pour itself out into a receptacle"). In "I am the hounded slave," the poet's self-doubling flushes nouns and verbs alike into physicality: *hounded, wince, despair, crack, clutch, gore, ooze, fall.* The poet's language also plays with the directional possibilities (right to left, left to right) of his fused identities: not only does the physical body arise to become the floating phantom, but the phantom's agonies (its immaterial woundings) can reverse into material furnishings (the garments he wears):

> Agonies are one of my changes of garments,
> I do not ask the wounded person how he feels, I myself
>   become the wounded person,
> My hurts turn livid upon me as I lean on a cane and
>   observe.

In simultaneous actions, the wounded body bleeds as the phantom bleeds, immaterially, invisibly, while the immaterial body, livid with hidden hurts, issues from the apparently unharmed observer leaning on his cane. Standing in the street, the supposed "observer" absents himself into a "fluid" new state of feeling. Whitman's most eloquent and indubitable testimony to the mysterious process by which self-effusion generates an immaterial identity appears in a sublime moment of the prose Preface to *Leaves of Grass*. There effusion is described in almost biblical cadences, because even to the poet himself the invisible (but entirely real) psychological "effusing" seems an almost miraculous phenomenon:

> From the eyesight proceeds another eyesight and from the hearing proceeds another hearing and from the voice proceeds another voice eternally curious of the harmony of things with man.

OWING TO his interest in others, and because he could "effuse" himself into almost anyone, in "The Artillery-man's Vision" Whitman invents, so far as I know, the first American poem of PTSD. Gradually, in his involuntary effusion of linguistic sympathy into the mind of the Artilleryman, Whitman diagnoses the soldier's affliction as a form of mental illness with a tragic prognosis: the soldier cannot (in the world of the poem) awaken from his postwar "vision" and rejoin his sleeping family. The poem is not the history of a single flashback (defined as "a reawakened memory"). On the contrary, through its bizarre structures and disorganized suites of perceptions, it becomes a surreal portrait of the grim alterations of a disturbed mind.

It also incarnates Wordsworth's aphoristic but less familiar definition of poetry in his note to "The Thorn" (for the 1800 edition of *Lyrical Ballads*): "Poetry is passion: it is the history or science of feelings." The poem's irregular narrative "plot" furnishes the *history* of the Artilleryman's heightened senses and hypervigilant feelings, while the incoherent orientations of his "vision" bring to light Whitman's *science* of the feelings aroused by the distress of reliving—not merely remembering—the trauma of witnessing or participating in death-threatening events. I am not the first to see the poem as a description of PTSD, but critics, in their abbreviated mention of the plot, tend to treat the "vision" as a flashback to an actual memory of a single event, a literal transcription of real sights seen by day. But the Artilleryman calls the "sight" that shocks him awake not a memory or a nightmare, but a "vision"—a sacred word, denoting a transcendent and involuntary revelation.

Whitman must bring his readers to recognize the Artilleryman's "vision" not as a realistic transcript of the seen but rather as a record of the motions of a suffering mind—as a form of mental illness. How do we come to judge the Artilleryman's "vision" as a form of mental disease inducing distortion and distraction? The poem's disorder matches, I believe, one variety of the psychological disorders now medically defined (not least in the DSM) under the term "Post-Traumatic Stress Disorder" as a response to having experienced or witnessed actual or threatened death. Unafraid of diagnosing the Artilleryman's symptoms as indicators of a mental illness, Whitman establishes a tragic prognosis by violating the presumptive "happy ending" of such a poem. Normally an opening frame is matched by a closing frame, and since the soldier was asleep before being awakened by his "vision" we expect him to make a successful return from the vision-journey to his domestic bedroom. This he does not do. By amputating the expected exit-frame, Whitman traps his soldier in permanent trauma.

There are, I would say, three plots to "The Artillery-man's Vision." The first is the external, asymmetrical, and tragic plot of the frame-lacking-its-end-frame, which consigns the Artilleryman to everlasting torment. From his night-watches in hospital wards, Whitman would have known that post-traumatic stress could give rise to a recurrent disorder, warranting a hopeless closure of his poem. The second plot, the one of external narrative, tracks the battle's sights and sounds as the Artilleryman's mind renders them, while silently, by various manipulations of language, it unveils the effects of trauma on his perceptions, exhibiting the full terror and zest of war before the "vision" arrives at its increasingly chaotic and dangerous close. And the third plot—initially invisible and most inventive—is that of the gradual dehumanization of the Artilleryman by the hellish elements of the "vision" pressing upon him.

In World War I, the link between unendurable battles and the nervous collapse of some soldiers seemed self-evident, requiring for healing only a period of sustained rest, after which the soldier was to be sent back to the front. (Success in "healing" was erratic.) Physicians attempting, at Craiglockhart Hospital, to treat Wilfred Owen, Siegfried Sassoon, and other sufferers laid a groundwork for the scientific study of the disease. More recently, the internal and therefore invisible psychic injuries common in PTSD, such as "derealization" (in which the external world appears unreal) and "dissociation" (in which the sufferer watches himself from a numbed distance), have been added to the more evident behavioral symptoms (agitation, tremor, insomnia, self-isolation, hostility, and sudden flashbacks). "The Artilleryman's Vision" is Whitman's early—and astonishingly accurate—example of the variety of PTSD that, as an internal mental disease, is harbored invisibly by a physically uninjured veteran.

We notice immediately a disjunctive feature of "The Artilleryman's Vision": a hidden third-person "external" narrator gives the poem its title, thereby introducing his human subject not by a personal name but by a military title establishing the soldier's battle-function: he is the Artilleryman. (We soon discover that all the active soldiers in the poem are identified solely by their military functions.) The title-announcer does not call the poem "I, the Artilleryman"; rather, he is himself a military officer categorizing his men by their assigned mission. After the title, the Artilleryman immediately "takes over" the poem in his deceptively serene first-person opening lines, which serve to frame the central "vision" of battle. As the narrative proper arrives, the ex-soldier (at home) suddenly wakes explosively into a "vacant" midnight which is involuntarily and immediately "filled" by battle-scenes ("I see") and sounds ("I hear"). The poem then tracks the soldier's increasingly violent responses to his battle-vision. At first the Artilleryman strives to retain a frail residual sanity, recognizing his vision as a "fantasy unreal"; in a second phase (the battle) he strives to organize his perceptions by several means, for instance by connecting weapons and their wielders, but is defeated by the battle's overwhelming number of details pressing to be classified; in the third, noise and chaos mount as he undergoes a form of exhilarating madness, bearing out Whitman's most penetrating insight—that it is "the old mad joy" of killing that floods the heart of the now dehumanized soldier.

Whitman is of course not the first lyric poet brave enough to give a poetic journey an unhappy ending.

George Herbert dared, in "The Pilgrimage," to thwart the devoted traveler's arrival at his sacred destination. When the pilgrim finds, as he ends his journey, not the promised "gladsome hill" but only "a lake of brackish waters," he cries out,

> Alas my King!
> Can both the way and end be tears?

It is a beautiful and resentful line, and as the deceived pilgrim journeys on, he observes that any rest, even that of death, would be preferable to this dangerous and unjust form of life:

> After so foul a journey death is fair,
>   And but a chair.

Although Herbert's pilgrim is allowed at least that closing complaint, Whitman's Artilleryman at the end disappears, completely unable to depart from the horrors by which he is still surrounded. Robbed of his personal functions, he is fixed forever in his military one.

Whitman was troubled as he sought for a truthful conclusion to "The Artilleryman's Vision." We know this because he left a draft of the poem from 1862 called "A Battle." There the Artilleryman addresses an anonymous comrade, narrating the events that he sees. In the immediate aftermath of mass killing, however, he cannot continue his "objective" description of the battle, whereupon his recital falls apart in his hands. Mid-line, his third-person narration leaps into first-person testimony, sliding from fact into personal outcry:

The chief gunner ranges and sights his piece, and
      selects a fuse of the right time,
(After a shot, see how he leans aside and looks eagerly
      off, to see the effect!)
Then after the battle, what a scene! O my sick soul,
      how the dead lie.

The first-person draft-lament accelerates into an uncon-
trolled tautology of melodrama:

O the hideous damned hell of war
Were the preachers preaching of hell?
O there is no hell more damned than this hell of war.
O what is here? O my beautiful young men! O the
      beautiful hair, clotted! The faces!

But almost immediately Whitman rejected the draft:
apparently he could not feel at home in his own sedu-
lously inserted but emotionally arid intrusions ("After
a shot, see how he leans aside and looks eagerly off, to
see the effect!"), nor could he accept the unravelling of
his lament into incoherent repetition. In 1865, when the
abandoned draft was revised into first-person enuncia-
tion, the poet found a chillingly fitting form of closure,
as we shall see.

Whitman had been asking himself whether he, as a
non-combatant, has a right to speak in a soldier's voice.
In the draft he had hoped that addressing a "you" would
insert some second-person drama into the poem while
wondering why he was unable to animate a third-person
narrative. As the finished poem reveals, he solved the prob-
lem of voice by capitulating altogether to a first-person
voice emanating from an active soldier. In this capitulation

he is obeying the injunctions of poetic law in preference to personal fact. Speaking always, now, as the Artilleryman, Whitman will "become" a combatant, and his feelings (as well as his observations) will, as Wordsworth prescribed, govern his language.

Manifestations of feelings throughout the battle-scenes in the finished poem are multiple. In "A Battle," the soldier uses verbal nouns (nouns made from verbs, and therefore more stable than verbs) in performing his inventory of weapons: he hears not bombs buzzing or muskets rattling, but rather abstractions: "the hum and buzz of the great shells . . . the rattle of musketry." Such a conversion establishes the passage of time and gives distinct attention to each weapon. But finally the Artilleryman gives up on his inventory, despairing of precision and falling into vaguely generalized groups ("the sounds of the different missiles") such as haunt his "vision." Forsaking words, he valiantly attempts phonetic mimicry ("the short *t-h-t! t-h-t!* of the rifle-balls"), falling back on such aural transcription once more in the penultimate line. Hoping to find a vein by which he may be able to "effuse" and empower himself, the Artilleryman internally undergoes the impact of his vision, unprepared for its outcome. At first a sliver of sanity remains, as the soldier characterizes his vision as a "fantasy unreal" and can adopt an "objective" view: "The skirmishers begin," "tumultuous now the contest rages." But such distanced perception disappears as the Artilleryman reenters the battle, flaunting his imaginative power with hyperbole: "*All* the scenes at the batteries" return again.

But in what manner do all the scenes arise? The Artilleryman's view must now be a panoramic one (a form of divine omniscience) in sound as well as sight: the orchestral noise-level rises ominously. Whitman must conjure up—and represent—how the "vision" of a PTSD sufferer differs from the "same" events as seen in ordinary life or in transcriptive memory. He continues to imagine and to re-create the world as it lies inside the oppressed Artilleryman's brain—distorted, arbitrarily condensed, irrationally contracted or expanded in the fantasy of the "vision." To the startled Artilleryman, his "fantasy unreal" has become altogether real. The "vision" dictates even his cognition, what the soldier sees and where he directs his glance.

We perceive, as the soldier sketches his scenes, the flagrant reductiveness of war. The soldiers are nothing but their functions: stripped of their personal names and their domestic roles, they become faceless individuals, unranked, without identifying uniforms, socially naked until they are given their guns and uniforms and their assignments or rank—"the chief-gunner," "the colonel." When the Artilleryman sees a group of nameless "men" not yet engaged in battle, proudly exhibiting their guns, he offers no details of their position, rank, or duties; they participate in the facelessness of "the ranks." The new recruits remain nameless until they acquire, along with their uniforms and their guns, a military identity, an identifiable place in the army's implacable hierarchy. Thus does the Artilleryman's "vision" become "unreal," deleting from its soldiers all identifications but the external ones that they acquire when they join the army, becoming replaceable cogs in the military machine. If one artilleryman falls, another can be called to take his place.

I MUST MENTION, because it clarifies the unexpected closure of "The Artilleryman's Vision," another draft (immediately following the draft of "A Battle"), which will evolve into "A March in the Ranks Hard-Prest, and the Road Unknown." In it, Whitman finds a plausible way to insert a first-person soliloquy into a third-person poem: one soldier, detaching himself from troops briefly resting from their "hard-prest" march fleeing their defeat, enters a field-hospital full of wounded and dying soldiers. Sharp-eyed, the soldier details all that he observes, arriving finally at the most desperate sight, a death-spasm. A reader may be baffled by the very strange end to the soldier's soliloquy: after he turns back to rejoin the ranks, the last sight that he records from his time in the field-hospital has nothing expressly to do with the wounded and dying. Rather, he notes a purely eye-catching aesthetic detail, "The glisten of the little steel instruments catching the flash of the torches." In the finished poem "flash" was removed and the line was revised to emphasize by alliteration the reciprocity of light from scale to scale, from "glisten" to "glint." The alliteration further magnetizes the two halves of the moving light-gestalt, creating in effect a fascinating "reverberation" of light in chiaroscuro across differences in scale, from great flashing torches to little steel instruments. I mention this involuntary distraction from pain—enabled by a diversion of the eye to an impersonal aesthetic notation—because such a diversion becomes indispensable to the unexpected conclusion of "The Artilleryman's Vision."

An old, reminiscing "artillerist" had turned up in the first edition of *Leaves of Grass* in 1855, but at that time Whitman had never seen war. By 1862, he evidently understood, from his work in the Washington hospitals, the intense suffering of men who appeared uninjured but who in fact bore invisible mental torments generated by what they and others had witnessed and done on the field. In Whitman's images of PTSD, the soldiers are not recovering "a" memory; rather, they are exposed to a kind of living film-mosaic of horrors accreted during their months or years of service. Their internal "film" has neither logic nor rational sequence, as Whitman is at pains to show in his "matching" of scenes to language.

When Whitman converts "The Artilleryman's Vision" into an autobiographical account, he makes sure, by its introductory peaceful domestic frame, that it is not a war poem but emphatically a postwar poem. It was first published under the title "The Veteran's Vision," but in 1871 the poet, realizing that it would be better understood as a poem about the psychic trauma of lethal battle, made his protagonist not merely a "veteran" but rather a soldier tasked to operate a large frontline cannon, and therefore inevitably responsible for many enemy deaths. Though the Artilleryman's initial battle details may sound "natural," the poet's language, by separating the sounds from each other and distributing them among distinct weapons, ensures the ongoing passage of time during his compelled and exhausting inventory. And by framing the Artilleryman's experience of battle not as a remembered past moment of war but as the "now" of private midnight aftereffects, Whitman has decided on a tragic prognosis for his wounded soldier.

The main verb of the Artilleryman's opening frame-narrative is in the present tense ("I wake"), and the apparently uninjured soldier alarmingly becomes a combatant again, filling the "vacant midnight" with his threatening "vision" as it unrolls through its "scenes" and "sounds," interspersed with early "objective" glimpses of the battle itself: "The skirmishers begin, they crawl cautiously ahead." These brief remarks reflect the soldier's attempt at the "objectivity" of a third-person observer. Soon enough, however, the aspiration to dispassionate reportage is crushed by the relentless vision that "presses upon" him, and he finds himself in the midst of a literally mimetic battle, where sounds substitute for words, and the soldier—still sane—comments parenthetically from the sidelines: "tumultuous now the contest rages!" The first-person voice will not, however, submit itself further to the impartial voice of detached observation. As the Artilleryman reenters the battle, he flaunts hyperbole as his banner of reprise: "all" the scenes at the batteries become present to him "again." "Again" is the familiar word normally introducing an imaginative reprise, except that here the alerted Artilleryman means the word literally. It is as though a curtain rises on an immense and overwhelming panorama of the entirety of his wartime experience and the vision must choose at each scene the point to which he must direct his glance.

As Whitman begins to imagine and re-create the world as it exists inside the oppressed Artilleryman's brain, experienced reality becomes distorted, arbitrarily condensed, irrationally contracted or expanded in the madness of "vision." To the startled Artilleryman, his private and obsessive "fantasy unreal" becomes, as it overcomes his resistance, an experience entirely real and relived. The chaos and increasing uncontrollability of the scenes as the battle progresses warn us that we are following, now, not reality but the deformities of thinking that haunt the veteran of the war. Normally, a narrator would create a reasonable chronology of the battle, but Whitman's Artilleryman produces scenes arbitrarily and at random: here a close-up, there a distance-view; here a sound, there an action; here a limited capacity, there a panoramic display. These scenes are not produced by the soldier but rather are "pressed" upon him like an incubus, as he lies passive under its rising undermining of rationality.

The poem's ever-unstated underplot is, as I say, that of the dehumanization of soldiers. The process, begun when the soldier was dislocated from his family and civilian life and reduced from being a named person to being a named function, can end only when the recruit returns home—but the Artilleryman can never return to "a normal life." The dense battle in his "vision" is similarly reduced, since it is "populated" by only two groups: soldiers and weapons. The weapons-as-independent-agents, "shrieking" and "bursting," dominate the Artilleryman's initial battle-scenes, and the killing power of those weapons excites their wielders. To the dehumanized "chief-gunner," his success in killing is a matter of skill, part of an athletic contest and not part of the shedding of blood. At various points in the vision, soldiers become caught up in their own success, and are cheering as though war were a sport, giving a "shout of applause" as if the battlefield were a theater. Slowly their dehumanization becomes undeniable. As fantasy becomes reality, the soldiers numb themselves against the realization of what they are actually doing.

War has so dehumanized the Artilleryman, so effaced human distinctions, that he enumerates fallen comrades only as "gaps cut by the enemy's volleys." The "gaps" (boasts the Artilleryman) are visually "quickly fill'd up, no delay." At first the Artilleryman was relatively remote from the center of the battle, dependent on the senses that can operate at a distance, on sight and hearing, but as the battle closes in on him, a nearer sense is activated as his nostrils must admit "the suffocating smoke." After the respite of a deceptive "lull," the Artilleryman—earlier the active listener to what he was hearing but now an assaulted victim—quails before "the chaos louder than ever." The density of the population on the field increases: close by, he hears "eager calls and orders of officers," who are, we suppose, as "eager" as the chief-gunner to see the effect of their weapons. And all of these scenes have a soundtrack: "And ever the sound of the cannon far or near." Enemy cannon like his own now approach the Artilleryman; he cannot escape their menace.

At this desperate point Whitman's genius comes most fully into play: the last word we expect to hear from the Artilleryman is "joy." Yet here it is, as Whitman penetrates to the ultimate heart of war: it is a primitive tribal savagery, permitted nowhere else in "civilized" life. Not only is it a "joy," but it is also a madness—an "old" madness recognized from some previous undefined violence perpetrated by the Artilleryman himself on some victim. Whitman's boldest insight is the frighteningly intimate response of "joy" to violence. In the depths of his soul the Artilleryman feels "a devilish exultation and all the old mad joy." The Artilleryman still has a conscience, he still knows his joy to be "devilish," but in the grip of his vision he is immune to shame and guilt. From the indifference of the soldier to the bodies that fill the gap in the line, from the dehumanization of the soldier until he is nothing but a weapon of war, feeling wild joy as his cannon leaps into action, Whitman depicts the Artilleryman's moral dissolution as he ignores his own companions, wounded unto death, as they flee the front. Indeed, self-numbed against the truth, he boasts of his own insensibility: "The falling, dying, I heed not, the wounded dripping and red I heed not, some to the rear are hobbling."

"And ever the sound of the cannon . . . And ever the hastening infantry shifting positions." "Ever" is the summary word of the vision; the Artilleryman is powerless to expel his incubus. How is it, then, that the Artilleryman turns his eyes skyward at the end? He is still in his "vision," but he is deflecting guilt and shame by two methods: he sophistically displays his "patriotism" by quoting from Francis Scott Key's poem "Defence of Fort M'Henry" (later set to the music of an English tavern song on its way to becoming our national anthem, "The Star-Spangled Banner"), and he resorts to an aesthetic language to support his evasion, resembling the soldier in "A March in the Ranks Hard-Prest, and the Road Unknown" who could no longer bear to focus on comrades dying and focused instead on "glints" picked up by small steel instruments from the "glisten" of the great torches. Since the artist's eye seeks out from childhood what is beautiful, there is always the temptation (especially in youth) to obscure the unacceptable and to mask it by some version of the beautiful. The most courageous artists, like Whitman in "The Artilleryman's Vision," hope to refuse the temptation to aestheticize, and therein to falsify, the truth.

THE ARTILLERYMAN'S VISION never releases him: Whitman refuses to return him to the slumbering wife and the breathing infant of the opening frame. In the last moment of his vision, he is still trapped in the hell of war; there is no homecoming from derangement. The soldier attempts to sanitize his vision by abstracting it, in its last words, into a purely visual epiphenomenon: "and at night the vari-color'd rockets." Yet he does not succeed, by these self-exculpations, in escaping his vision; it is still in power, still "pressing upon" its victim, enabling the Artilleryman to excuse his violent joy in war by concluding on an "innocent" and unrepentant note, pleased by the distance from himself in Key's poetic bombs and colored rockets in the sky. It is a self-defensive conclusion that should shock every reader, the Artilleryman's flight, by means of an appeal to isolated beauty, from the deaths inflicted on others by his cannon.

To confine a battle to a short lyric is to court trouble. It is natural in a war poem to cite a *casus belli,* but in the published poem Whitman does not. The implications are evident. What are the two sides fighting about? Who knows, who cares; war is a constant in every culture; men, weapons, deaths. What permits war? The dehumanization of the soldiers on both sides. And what motivates war, generation after generation? Exhilaration: men find it exhilarating, a unique, irresponsible thrill, and can forget, in its spell, the humanity not only of their opponents but of their fellow-soldiers, even of themselves.

Only after rereading "The Artilleryman's Vision" do we recognize its analytic ambition: to diagnose, silently, by the apparently incoherent reportage of the postwar mentality of a flailing soldier, a disordered mind helpless against the midnight assaults of its alternately frightful and (secretly) zestful vision. And it is only after seeing the poem as a case history that we recognize the implicit prognosis in its abrupt end. Within his own stricken account, the Artilleryman cannot diagnose his case or admit its prognosis. Every conclusion drawn by the reader must be hinted at by Whitman's pen—whether by a structural feature (the absence of a closing "frame"); a fall into mimetic sound to suggest the impossibility of intelligible renditions of battle; an unnerving descent into a suddenly religious vocabulary—"the depths of my soul"—when the Artilleryman is appalled by his own appetite for killing, his "devilish exultation and all the old mad joy." And the more frenzied revelation—"I heed [them] not"—allows us to see him indeed as a damned soul, further damned by his affected distance as he contemplates not death or dehumanization or self-numbing but instead the pleasing liveliness of the skyward spectacle. And by the time he fuses, at the end, an illogical list of unregulated entities—"Grime, heat, rush, aide-de camps galloping by"—we perceive that his mind has broken down into a distorting chaos from which he will never recover, a recurrent mental illness not yet given a name.

Can Poetry Be Abstract?

[*No coward soul is mine*]

No coward soul is mine
No trembler in the world's storm-troubled sphere
I see Heaven's glories shine
And Faith shines equal arming me from Fear

O God within my breast
Almighty ever-present Deity
Life, that in me hast rest
As I Undying Life, have power in thee

Vain are the thousand creeds
That move men's hearts, unutterably vain,
Worthless as withered weeds
Or idlest froth amid the boundless main

To waken doubt in one
Holding so fast by thy infinity
So surely anchored on
The steadfast rock of Immortality

With wide-embracing love
Thy spirit animates eternal years
Pervades and broods above,
Changes, sustains, dissolves, creates and rears

Though Earth and moon were gone
And suns and universes ceased to be
And thou wert left alone
Every Existence would exist in thee

There is not room for Death
Nor atom that his might could render void
Since thou art Being and Breath
And what thou art may never be destroyed

EMILY BRONTË

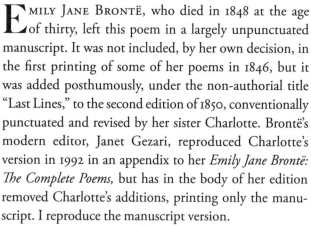

Emily Jane Brontë, who died in 1848 at the age of thirty, left this poem in a largely unpunctuated manuscript. It was not included, by her own decision, in the first printing of some of her poems in 1846, but it was added posthumously, under the non-authorial title "Last Lines," to the second edition of 1850, conventionally punctuated and revised by her sister Charlotte. Brontë's modern editor, Janet Gezari, reproduced Charlotte's version in 1992 in an appendix to her *Emily Jane Brontë: The Complete Poems,* but has in the body of her edition removed Charlotte's additions, printing only the manuscript. I reproduce the manuscript version.

Emily Dickinson, a few months before she died in 1886, wishing to forbid a church funeral, left instructions for a home funeral in which she stipulated that a single poem by Emily Brontë, "Last Lines," should be read aloud by her friend Thomas Wentworth Higginson, the editor of *The Atlantic Monthly.* Dickinson, reading the lines in 1850, considered them as Brontë's deathbed manifesto, and adopted them as her own final declaration of creedless faith. A certain Mrs. Jamison, who attended the funeral, recorded the fact that Higginson, prefacing his reading of "Last Lines" and of the scriptural passage that Dickinson had also stipulated to be read aloud (1 Corinthians 15:53, on immortality: "For this corruptible must put on

incorruption, and this mortal must put on immortality"),
remarked that Emily Dickinson had now put on immor-
tality, but she had really never seemed to have put it off.
I became interested in Brontë's poem when I first read
about Dickinson's funeral: I wanted to understand why,
out of the hundreds of poems known to Dickinson, she
had chosen this one as a vicarious final utterance of her
own.

"No coward soul is mine" has been "much commented
on," according to Janet Gezari, but although critics have
repeatedly tried to distill it into one creed or another
ascribable to Brontë—whose very aim was to escape
such fixed categories—no consensus has been attained.
"No coward soul is mine" is in part vividly definite, but
it is also sufficiently abstract to defy common conven-
tions of Christian lyric such as the inclusion of elements
of Jesus's life and sayings, allusions to church feasts and
rituals, and credal affirmation of an afterlife. The most
vigorous lines of Brontë's poem are those insisting on
the entirely interior nature of human faith: "Vain are the
thousand creeds / That move men's hearts, unutterably
vain." Brontë's "vain" is alluding not to vainglory but to
the opening chapter of Ecclesiastes: "Vanity of vanities,
saith the Preacher, vanity of vanities; all is vanity." The
Hebrew word translated into English as "vanity" is *hevel*,
and *hevel* (the commentaries tell us) is one of the several
Hebrew words for "air," or "wind," but is most often used
negatively to mean "fleeting," "transitory," "futile." Brontë
is speaking as a deeply literate nineteenth-century reader,
well aware (from the pre-Darwinian geological proof of
evolution) of the successive and transitory creeds of all
religions historically recorded.

For Brontë, Christianity—the only "creed" that she

knows well—must stand in for all other creeds and their myths of a divinity both creative and inspiring; and Brontë must invent her own version of the sublime phenomenon of unbidden human inspiration. She does it most conspicuously in this poem. It must be remembered that Brontë was the daughter of a learned priest of the English Church, an Oxford graduate in classics, himself a poet, whose children were raised as Christian believers, and who all (except Emily) taught in his Sunday school. Brontë's poetic duty in denying the truth of "creeds" is to strip the Christian God of every sustainable predicate. Theologians had asserted at least since Aquinas, following Maimonides, that no positive qualities could be predicated of God, owing to the limitations of language: He (always male) could be characterized only negatively, as one who was *not* subject to death, *not* affected by time, *not* vulnerable to suffering. This affirmation became known as apophatic theology. God was im-mortal, e-ternal, im-passible.

Brontë's own "Deity" is an internal one, replacing the external and mythological God of the creeds and taking on an ever-present existence within herself, to be interpreted only by herself. The relation between self and Deity, as Brontë formulates it, is a perfect and cunningly phrased closed circuit of reciprocity. Addressing her Deity as a lowercase "thou" to her "I," Brontë poises their relation as one of mutually acknowledged parallel acts of repose and empowerment as she addresses her Deity: "Life, that in me hast rest / As I Undying Life, have power in thee." Her Deity, a capitalized "Undying Life," accepts a physical repose within herself as she exists in its Life, receiving power as she participates in its immortal "Undying" metaphysical existence.

This Deity is neither anthropomorphized nor given gender; it displays no external acts such as Adamic creation and is embodied in no human figure such as Jesus. It is a presence, not a person, and its sole activity is its never-lapsing "wide-embracing love." This unconfined love, Brontë writes, *shines* as powerfully as "Heaven's glories" *shine*. The use of the identical verb "shine" for both nouns establishes the identity of past Christian myth—the capitalized "Heaven's glories"—and Brontë's internal inspiration, the "wide-embracing love." This love is neither *eros* nor *agape*, but rather an intuited third possibility: a love that within the visionary seer temporarily annihilates historical time and replaces it with Eternity. The poet's own conviction is fiercely declared: she surveys all doctrinal codifications only to scorn them. "Vain are the . . . creeds of men." Since Christianity, the only religion known to her, is credal (from the Latin *credo*, "I believe"), Brontë, with one wipe of the sponge, erases all such doctrines, and dares to propose that the intermittently self-revealing "God within [her] breast" differs from any religious figure, such as Jesus, who enacts a fixed identity within a fictional narrative.

Brontë's God here is not a trinity. It at first occupies one half of a duality of absence and presence: her ordinary self has access to her Deity only when she is unexpectedly and involuntarily admitted to a presence suffusing her with indwelling inspiration. Only then is she able to address her "thou." Instead of projecting her inspiration outwardly on an allegorical figure such as the Muse, Brontë strikingly makes inspiration indistinguishable from her own physical Being and bodily Breath. She realizes that, in the disbelief of the mid-nineteenth century, a new "rational" and sober manner of addressing the divine must reject Christian elements elaborated in sacraments and rituals. A mention of Jesus? The birth at Bethlehem? The Passion? Holy Communion? No.

We can better understand the poetic paradox of a "spiritual" rhetoric uninhabited by religious images and narratives by remembering one of Emily Dickinson's more acerbic remarks about God. Writing to Higginson about her family as she listens to their daily morning family prayers full of unverifiable language, she explains: "They are religious, except me – and address an Eclipse, every morning – whom they call their 'Father.'" How could a poet address an eclipse?

As usual, Dickinson sees the conceptual problem as one of language: given the erasure by the eclipse of all information concerning light articulated in Hebrew or Christian diction, from "Let there be light" (Genesis 1:3) to Jesus's saying "I am the light of the world" (John 8:12), what words would the poet be able to use? Deprived of light, life is merely an eventual eclipse of ourselves. In 1863, in her poem "We dream – it is good we are dreaming," Life is a malevolent executioner hunting its prey: "[Life] is playing – kill us, / And we are playing – shriek –." Dickinson is macabre, whereas Brontë is ecstatic, but the problem of the articulation of the human sublime—what will be its diction and its tonality?—is common to both poets. In 1864, a year after "playing – shriek," Dickinson exposes nakedly her own version of the death of God:

> Truth – is as old as God –
> His Twin identity
> And will endure as long as He
> A Co-Eternity –

And perish on the Day
Himself is borne away
From Mansion of the Universe
A lifeless Deity.

Like Brontë, by whose strategies she was doubtless inspired, Dickinson thought long and hard about retaining enough sacred reference to make clear that she was engaged in stripping the Christian God of all supernatural credibility. Dickinson capitalizes, here, the "sacred" word "Mansion" to reveal her allusion to the Christian belief in an afterlife. She is quoting Jesus's promise as he bids farewell to his apostles: "In my Father's house are many mansions: if it were not so, I would have told you" (John 14:2). Yet how are the poets to retain a devotional tone while deleting from it any overt reference to theology, ritual, and religious narrative? How is the object of worship to be made convincingly abstract and yet able to install reverence by its (hidden) Christian allusions and a tone of veneration?

Emily Brontë, born in 1818, was older by only twelve years than Dickinson, but she and her sisters Charlotte and Anne, who had jointly published under three pseudonyms in 1846, were known to Dickinson. In 1860, five years after the last of the sisters, Charlotte Brontë ("Currer Bell"), died, Dickinson elegized her as a singing Nightingale now caged in its grave, presenting her as a poet rather than as a novelist:

All overgrown by cunning moss,
All interspersed with weed,

> The little cage of "Currer Bell"
> In quiet "Haworth" laid.

Emily, closer in sensibility to Dickinson, had died at thirty, too early for an elegy by Dickinson, but in representing Charlotte as a poet-nightingale rather than as a novelist, one might think of her as embodying Emily. (Charlotte and Emily are buried in Haworth in a single grave bearing a joint gravestone.)

In an appendix to Richard Sewall's biography of Dickinson, there is a useful supplement collecting poems by American women on topics akin to those of Dickinson: Love, Death, Time, Nature, Art. They disclose the sentimentality and cliché that Dickinson in maturity was so determined to avoid (or to mock as "Dimity Convictions"), and it is unthinkable that Dickinson could have turned to such poets in choosing a surrogate literary voice for her funeral. Her own reading in poetry was chiefly from the English poets. She mentions "Mrs. Browning" (with several references to *Aurora Leigh,* Elizabeth Barrett Browning's feminist novel-in-verse) and George Eliot (the novels, not the poems), but there is no recorded response to Christina Rossetti (whose mournful Christian verse is far from Dickinson's briskness). Barrett Browning turned increasingly to political verse in her later Italian years, making her a less inviting model for Dickinson. Among contemporary women poets, Dickinson found only in Emily Brontë a kindred spirit as irreligious as herself, as highly educated, as outspoken and as fearless in unambiguous statement: "No coward soul is mine," "Vain are the thousand creeds that move men's hearts." Each of these declarations by Brontë would not be out of place in a poem by Dickinson. Dickinson could have chosen something by Browning or Tennyson, but in choosing a woman poet Dickinson defined herself against Brontë's collective ideological men proclaiming successively their vain "thousand creeds."

In ventriloquizing Brontë's "Last Lines," Dickinson identified to her mourners an early example of the post-Christian religious lyric, unafraid of its secular stance, bold in its purity. As Dickinson perceived with instant indebtedness, Brontë had invented a form of poem that rejected Christianity but had nowhere else to turn for tonal models of worship, gratitude, and consolation except to Christian lyric. Brontë had had to find a way of verbal divestment, a genuine means by which she could both summon and address her secular "Deity." Luckily, Brontë knew Milton's address to "holy light" as "Bright effluence of bright essence increate," which had pointedly used extreme abstraction as a way of representing the divine.

The young Keats, in the "Ode to Psyche," had taken on the problem later faced by Brontë—how to write devotionally after the death of the gods—but he had decided that the solution lay in an exact interior (mental) replication of Psyche's Greek cult-forms. He takes a solemn vow:

> Yes, I will be thy priest, and build a fane
>> In some untrodden region of my mind,
> Where branched thoughts, new grown with pleasant pain,
>> Instead of pines shall murmur in the wind[.]

By making an exact mental replica of the cult, Keats clears away Psyche's Greek worship and makes his modern mental shrine exactly match the ancient external one, in the hope that the goddess will come to inhabit it. Brontë will not succumb to such a mimesis of past cultic practice: instead she evacuates from Christian poetry its former content, detaching its words from their roots in fable, sacred texts, and personal symbol. In "No coward soul is mine," she uses words immemorially familiar from their Christian contexts—*soul, Heaven, Faith, God, Almighty, Deity, Undying Life, infinity, Immortality, spirit, eternal*— but they appear nakedly, as if extracted from a contextless dictionary of theological vocabulary. We do not hear of the biblical narratives from which *rock* and *anchor* have been detached; we know only that an unnamed Deity is "Holding so fast by thy infinity" and "anchored on / The steadfast rock of Immortality." Everything in Brontë is invisible.

Brontë must have known the most frightening abstract poem of Romanticism, Coleridge's "Constancy to an Ideal Object," where, after conveying the sadness and bleakness of a purposeless life which constantly yearns for an Ideal Object worthy of lasting love, he savagely denies (while preserving its beauty) the eternal delusion prompting such a yearning. An Ideal Object is not a something; it is a nothing. Addressing the impossible Ideal Object, Coleridge, closing his poem, displays to the Ideal Object, by question and answer, its own vacancy of origin, while not suppressing its beauty:

> And art thou nothing? Such thou art, as when
> The woodman winding westward up the glen
> At wintry dawn, where o'er the sheep-track's maze
> The viewless snow-mist weaves a glist'ning haze,
> Sees full before him, gliding without tread,
> An image with a glory round its head;

The enamored rustic worships its fair hues,
Nor knows he makes the shadow, he pursues!

Words in many of Brontë's poems remain apparently
intelligible only because the mind hears in them echoes
of past belief, but the echoes fade as they are replaced by a
paradoxical and living web of active creative verbs, prob-
ably borrowed (as her editor suggests) from Coleridge's
famous description in *Biographia Literaria* of the "second-
ary" imagination, the first imagination being that of the
Creator. (It was in truth Coleridge's own human imagina-
tion that he was exploring, just as his first title-choice was
Autobiographia Literaria.) His Latinate verbs are interiorly
and etymologically complex: "It dissolves, diffuses, dissi-
pates, in order to recreate . . . it struggles to idealize and to
unify. It is essentially *vital*." Coleridge insists that the ever-
changing and vital human imagination must "dissolve"
before it can "recreate."

Brontë's "wide-embracing love" similarly "dissolves"
and then "creates" itself in a vital form that not only "ani-
mates" but also, in the end, "rears" itself into a positive
absolute:

Thy spirit animates eternal years
Pervades and broods above,
Changes, sustains, dissolves, creates and rears[.]

The reader must restore individual etymological or allu-
sive content to each of Brontë's eight verbs, as I indicate
by my added bracketed phrases below: *Thy spirit animates*
[bestows an active individual soul upon impersonal eter-
nal] *years*; *Thy spirit pervades* [diffuses itself, like a vapor, in
every direction]; *Thy spirit broods above* [as an incubating

bird], just as in Luke 13:34 Jesus wishes he could have gathered up the children of Jerusalem "as a hen doth gather her brood under her wings." Brontë's changes of focus—and their invisible sustaining metaphors, as in my bracketed "completions" above—rapidly accumulate in the five verbs of her final line. And later, Dickinson, out-doing both Coleridge and Brontë, introduces an unstoppable cascade of verbs into her own poem on "The Love a Life can show Below," where, at the ending, in a heap of twelve verbs, lifelong love on earth "dissolves" only so that it can return in Paradise:

> 'Tis this – invites – appalls – endows –
> Flits – glimmers – proves – dissolves –
> Returns – suggests – convicts – enchants
> Then – flings in Paradise –

The poet resorts to such excited abstractions to depict a world from which a changeless God has departed, making life narratable only as a succession of unpredictable and shifting perceptions. Like Brontë's rock and anchor, Dickinson's unstable actions are removed from a person, a situation, and a coherent narrative line. Her poem makes uninterpretable kaleidoscopic turns—here, love glimmers; there, it convicts; and elsewhere, it provides a proof.

To INVENT a daring abstract language which worships an internal Deity while forsaking a causal event, a stable narrative, a restored myth, and a theological intelligibility in favor of detachment, abstraction, and personal ecstasy, is a cultural novelty in English verse which subsequent non-religious poets, reading Brontë, can understand, investigate, imitate, and adopt for their own purposes.

Since Brontë designs her own abstract language to imitate the aspirational or grieving tones and yearning of Christian lyric discourse, her twenty-first-century readers can scarcely perceive how relentlessly she eviscerates it of doctrinal or mythical or cultic content. The hope, calm, peace, and harmony of Brontë's inner ecstatic vision—and the agony of its departure as the human senses reawaken—arrive most precisely in the hexameters of "The Prisoner," in which the struggling imprisoned visionary-in-chains is each night soothed by Hope's "Mute music" in a dawning of the Invisible:

'But, first, a hush of peace—a soundless calm descends;
The struggle of distress, and fierce impatience ends.
Mute music soothes my breast, unuttered harmony,
That I could never dream, till Earth was lost to me.

'Then dawns the Invisible; the Unseen its truth reveals;
My outward sense is gone, my inward essence feels:
Its wings are almost free—its home, its harbour found,
Measuring the gulf, it stoops, and dares the final bound.'

But the success of that final leap is prevented by the involuntary reawakening of the senses:

'Oh, dreadful is the check—intense the agony—
When the ear begins to hear, and the eye begins to see;
When the pulse begins to throb, the brain to think
    again,
The soul to feel the flesh, and the flesh to feel the chain.'

The poet's hexameters become tragic as the rising momentum of vision is lost, and the soul becomes fixed in the immobile and inexorable syntax of ordinary sense-life, physical and mental and spiritual dullness, and biological despair:

When	the ear	begins to hear
and	the eye	begins to see;
When	the pulse	begins to throb,
	the brain	to think again,
	The soul	to feel the flesh
and	the flesh	to feel the chain.

Such a passage reproduces the abysmal sensation of involuntarily resuming a physical and mental and spiritual existence lacking all divine colloquy, the chain locks shut on the sequence "feel . . . flesh . . . flesh . . . feel."

After its former displays of ecstatic relief from pain, Brontë's former duality of flesh and spirit in "The Prisoner" grimly encounters in "The Philosopher" a baleful inner Trinity, ever in mutual conflict:

> Three gods, within this little frame,
> Are warring night and day;
> Heaven could not hold them all, and yet
> They all are held in me[.]

Brontë's triply conflicted self is redefined by the apparently desirable image of a spirit standing within the flow of three rivers, one golden, one like blood, and one like sapphire (perhaps desire, will, and tears), but in the end they all helplessly "tumbled in an inky sea." The speaker, immersed in that marine darkness, recalls its hellish effect: "Oh, let me die—that power and will / Their cruel strife may close." The famously tenacious Brontë will continues fiercely to will, but remains without power to act, and decides on suicide. It is the deepest feminist cry of Victorian poetry, in which an immense will to create can find no outlet in publication.

Bronte's intimations of thwarted vision continue in Hardy's "The Darkling Thrush," composed on December 31, 1900, and originally titled "At the Century's Death-Bed." In it, the poet unwillingly admits that the full-throated song of an aged male thrush seems to hope for an emotional vitality at present inaccessible to the depressed sixty-year-old poet:

> An aged thrush, frail, gaunt, and small,
>   In blast-beruffled plume,
> Had chosen thus to fling his soul
>   Upon the growing gloom.
>
> So little cause for carolings
>   Of such ecstatic sound
> Was written on terrestrial things
>   Afar or nigh around,
> That I could think there trembled through
>   His happy good-night air
> Some blessed Hope, whereof he knew
>   And I was unaware.

Unwilling to abandon his momentary participation in the thrush's hope, the atheist Hardy has nestled it (in Bronte's fashion) in the retained diction of Christianity (*soul, carolings, ecstatic, terrestrial, blessed, Hope*). To create true despair, Hardy needed only to write so as to contrast his depressive sentiment with the thrush's "happy . . . air," declaring that the thrush had ["Some blessed Hope

whereof he knew, / But I was unaware."] Yet Hardy adds
no comma and inserts an "And" instead of a "But," creat-
ing a true coordination between the thrush's firm knowing
and the speaker's (now perhaps remediable) unawareness.
Both Christmas and Twelfth Night bracket the century's
corpse, but narrative notice of Jesus's birth and the Three
Kings' mythical pilgrimage is, as in Brontë, absent.

The master of lyric abstraction, T. S. Eliot, composed
in 1927, just after his conversion, a brilliant lyric narrative
called "Journey of the Magi." It seems likely that he was
invisibly competing with his mother Charlotte's publica-
tion, in *The Christian Register* of Christmas 1887, a per-
fectly conventional, prosodically inept poem called "The
Three Kings." All its lines have four beats except for line 2
which has only three:

> "We are three kings who have traveled far,
>   O'er laced and sandy plain.
> Before us moved a radiant star,
>   Its light along our path is lain.
> Faint and weary, our journey's end
>   We seek, but the star moves onward still.
> We know not whither our footsteps tend,
>   Obedient to a higher will."

Eliot's poem draws on the seventeenth-century Christ-
mas sermon preached before King James by Lancelot
Andrewes, who uses the collective voice that Eliot adopts.
"Journey of the Magi" restricts its sole scriptural reference
(Matthew 2:1) to the word "Magi." The word first appears
in Jerome's first-century Christian Latin Vulgate to trans-
literate Matthew's Greek *magus*, meaning "a man learned
in arcane lore." The King James Version calls them "wise

men from the east," while the Catholic Douay-Rheims translation retains the Vulgate "Magi." Eliot presumably chooses the foreign word "Magi" in lieu of the KJV's "wise men" so that the poem will appear ancient and pre-Reformation in origin. (Neither translation specifies the number of the Magi; they acquired their number, names, and personalities from the accumulations of tradition; and their gifts, scriptural only by allusion to their source in Isaiah 60:6, enter Christianity also from tradition.) The gifts are not recorded in Matthew's Greek and remain unmentioned in Eliot's poem, so that the only item giving the poem any scriptural context is the single-word quotation from the Vulgate, "Magi," the barest of verbal references. Eliot is removing KJV familiarity—"wise men"—and making his title foreign and largely abstract—Journey of Whom?

Eliot's poem opens in a collective anonymous voice: "'A cold coming we had of it.'" We later discover that the tale of the journey is being recounted to, and recorded by, an amanuensis who appears only in the last stanza of the poem, as the voices, closing down the unhappy and unresolved account of their journey, command the recorder of their history to "set down / This set down / This." The poem intricately depicts a contest between a past journey recounted in the key of the definite article *the* and a set of arrivals recounted in the key of the indefinite article *a/an*. Here is a portion of the journey, which constantly repeats from lines 4 to 20 its specifying *the*:

> '*The* ways deep and *the* weather sharp,
>   *The* very dead of winter.'
> And *the* camels galled, sore-footed, refractory,
> Lying down in *the* melting snow.

> There were times we regretted
> *The* summer palaces on slopes, *the* terraces,
> And *the* silken girls bringing sherbet.

And here is a passage on arrival, pitched in the key of the repeated indefinite article *a* until its close, when it arrives at last at *the* prophesied place:

> Then at dawn we came down to *a* temperate valley . . .
> With *a* running stream and *a* water-mill . . .
> And *an* old white horse galloped away in the meadow.
> Then we came to *a* tavern . . .
> But there was no information, and so we continued
> And arrived at evening, not a moment too soon
> Finding *the* place; it was (you may say) satisfactory.

The arrival-landscape becomes allegorical of later events in the life of Jesus, meaningless of course to the journeying Magi: "three trees on the low sky . . . / Six hands at an open door dicing for pieces of silver."

The voices close the poem with a question to the amanuensis, fusing the two articles *the* and *a*—the latter not only for their first arrival at "a temperate valley," but also for their arrival back home after seeing "a Birth" and then, in the closing line, for their own envisaged third arrival— their longed-for personal death: "I should be glad of another death." Eliot adopts in this passage Brontë's strategy of capitalizing Sacred Things and using lowercase for human things, dramatizing the contrast most theatrically in the juxtaposition "like Death, our death," contrasting the implied sacred Crucifixion (the "three trees") and the Magi's human mortality.

were we led all that way for
Birth or Death? There was a Birth, certainly,
We had evidence and no doubt. I had seen birth and
    death,
But had thought they were different; this Birth was
Hard and bitter agony for us, like Death, our death.
We returned to our places, these Kingdoms,
But no longer at ease here, in the old dispensation,
With an alien people clutching their gods.
I should be glad of another death.

During their arduous journey, the Magi had sometimes
"regretted" their former worldly pleasures, always spec-
ified by *the*— "The summer palaces on slopes, the ter-
races, / And the silken girls bringing sherbet"—but after
their return to the East, the "palaces" are silently reduced
to mere "places" and the Magi find themselves with the
conundrum of their journey: was it a Birth they witnessed
or a Death? They cannot decide. All they know is that the
journey ruined the rest of their life.

JOHN ASHBERY finally brings Brontë's abstractions into
their full consequence. His book-length epic of abstract
narration called *Three Poems,* from 1972, evolves without
any religious support (although it allows allusion to any
number of canonical literary works, including the Bible).
The book is divided into three specifying parts: "The New
Spirit," "The System," and "The Recital," all dependent
on Eliot's work of specification in "Journey of the Magi,"
on Brontë's work in deleting Christian reference, and on
Dickinson's forthright substitution of Truth for Deity. It
also depends—and chiefly—on Yeats's tiny but defiant

poem announcing that the only accurate narrative of a life is the narration of its moods. Time decays as enlightenments come and go; both inorganic and organic nature change over geological time; but has any one of the eternal human moods ever been known to vanish?

The Moods

Time drops in decay,
Like a candle burnt out,
And the mountains and woods
Have their day, have their day;
What one in the rout
Of the fire-born moods
Has fallen away?

The obvious answer to Yeats's closing rhetorical question is "None." Human emotional and temperamental responses throughout life arrive as an uncontrollable "rout" (an unruly mob) of moods, generated not from the three temporal elements of the Greek world (Earth, Water, and Air) but rather from the fourth—and only immortal—realm, the celestial element of Fire. The form of Yeats's poem also supports the necessary answer: "None." We register the neat familiar logic of Yeats's rhymes—*decay, out, woods; day, rout, moods*—as we advance through the lyric because we recognize that he is constructing an English sixain: *abcabc.* Yet as we arrive at the end we are upset, because the poem, though it "should" stop at the sixth line, continues with an "extra" line, the seventh, which "restarts" the inexorable rhyme-chain with *away.* Yeats thereby displays the perpetual self-generating of the human moods in every human being from birth to death: the moods never subside, rout after rout of them.

If moods are the chief and perpetual inner events of human life—always and everywhere, appearing in our oldest oral and written literature and visual representations and preeminently in music—then as an artist records them, however incompletely or imperfectly, they become the most reliable narratives of our inner incessant responses to our infinitely conscious and unconscious life. To trace the moods has long been thought the special task of lyric, but Ashbery, by extending the mode to epic length in *Three Poems,* proposes that testimony to the moods is also the underlying work of all human narrative, even when it is presented novelistically or dramatically. Ashbery's long and sinuous ongoing sentences, influenced (as critics have noted) by the speculative novelists James and Proust, forsake the hard actualities of Homeric epic—a war, a journey—for a stylistic *tour de force*, a book-length exposition of the flickerings, doubts, convictions, affirmations, enjoyments, ecstasies, disappointments, and bafflements of the inner life. The moods are not structurally containable by human thought-systems. Ideology, shrinking and confining the human person into an idea-system, is, in this poetic, the enemy of human accuracy.

Three Poems is the modern equivalent of the Augustinian spiritual journals of the past, ever rising to a crest of faith or sinking into a trough of perplexity and despair, yet bound to remember what their author's fluctuating responses have amounted to in God's eyes, and to judge whether they are legitimate or unworthy. *Three Poems* (dedicated to the poet's partner David Kermani) is Ashbery's journal, moving through a haze of mist and fog, making inquiries into elementary particles of emotion and fugitive auroras, into intimations, into repudiations. Every new day arrives with irrepressible moods that tend to discard the old, distrust the new, cherish hopes, falter in confidence, and long for an idyll. The rout of moods never "solves" or "resolves" any life-question, because a new and thrilling disturbance of feeling will appear the moment the previous lapses into forgetfulness. Ashbery moves down the page always apparently in preparation for a contemplated undertaking, but is prevented by new inspirations or disbeliefs from any conclusive action. And there is no question of moral judgment of the self, because moods irrupt into being involuntarily.

A passage from *Three Poems* recording the moment of falling in love and discovering one's responses of shock and delight illustrates Ashbery's refusal of definiteness in favor of an abstract and equivocal (but finely shaded) balance of erotic delusion and erotic fulfillment, the latter causing the former. In the delusion of new love the world changes, and the lover becomes so suffused by emotion that he is certain that even insects and rodents must be feeling the glowing ambiance of desire:

> From the outset it was apparent that someone had played a colossal trick on something. The switches had been tripped, as it were; the entire world or one's limited but accurate idea of it was bathed in glowing love, of a sort that need never have come into being but was now indispensable as air is to living creatures. It filled up the whole universe, raising the temperature of all things. Not an atom but did not feel obscurely compelled to set out in search of a mate; not a living creature, no insect or rodent, that didn't feel the obscure twitchings of dormant love, that didn't ache to join in the universal turmoil and hullabaloo that fell over

the earth, roiling the clear waters of the reflective intellect, getting it into all kinds of messes that could have been avoided if only, as Pascal says, we had the sense to stay in our room, but the individual will condemns this notion and sallies forth full of ardor and *hubris,* bent on self-discovery in the guise of an attractive partner who is *the* heaven-sent one, the convex one with whom he has had the urge to mate all these seasons without realizing it.

In this abstract quasi-moral discourse from which everything moral has been deleted, we are left with the ultimately comic but also plangent dilemma of the poet whose every possibility remains (to quote Ammons's poem "Classic") "uncapturable and vanishing." *Three Poems,* unlikely ever to be exhausted, is equally unlikely to be imitated at such length and virtuosity, but it proves that even a long lyric narrative prose-poem can be fully abstract, appearing as the final extension of Brontë's abstract ventures in lyric.

Episode by episode, experiment by experiment, God has died on the poetic page, and has been replaced, as Dickinson prophesied, by a new Truth. A "scrawny cry from outside" (a scrawny bird-cry at dawn) is Stevens's description of the embryonic new truth in "Not Ideas About the Thing But the Thing Itself," but the poet predicts the reappearance of "the colossal sun, // Surrounded by its choral rings, / Still far away." Only posterity will know whether the scrawny cry of the abstract was a necessary move for the invention of a new poetics.

Sources and Works Cited

A. R. Ammons, *Bosh and Flapdoodle* (New York: W. W. Norton, 2005).

John Ashbery, *Collected Poems 1956–1987*, ed. Mark Ford (New York: Library of America, 2008).

William Blake, *The Poetry and Prose of William Blake*, ed. David V. Erdman (Garden City: Doubleday and Company, 1965).

——, *The William Blake Archive*, ed. Morris Eaves, Robert N. Essick, and Joseph Viscomi, 1993–, http://www.blake archive.org/.

Emily Jane Brontë, *Emily Jane Brontë: The Complete Poems*, ed. Janet Gezari (London and New York: Penguin, 1992).

Paul Celan, *Breathturn into Timestead: The Collected Later Poetry: A Bilingual Edition*, trans. Pierre Joris (New York: Farrar, Straus and Giroux, 2014).

William Cowper, *The Poems of William Cowper*, ed. John D. Baird and Charles Ryskamp, 3 vols. (Oxford: Clarendon Press, 1980–1995).

Leo Damrosch, *Eternity's Sunrise: The Imaginative World of William Blake* (New Haven: Yale University Press, 2015).

Emily Dickinson, *The Letters of Emily Dickinson*, ed. Cristanne Miller and Domhnall Mitchell (Cambridge, MA: Belknap Press of Harvard University Press, 2024).

——, *The Poems of Emily Dickinson: Reading Edition*, ed. R. W. Franklin (Cambridge, MA: Belknap Press of Harvard University Press, 1999).

John Donne, *The Complete English Poems of John Donne*, ed. C. A. Patrides (London: J. M. Dent & Sons Ltd, 1985).

T. S. Eliot, *The Poems of T. S. Eliot*, ed. Christopher Ricks and Jim McCue, 2 vols. (Baltimore: Johns Hopkins University Press, 2015).

Robert Hayden, *Collected Poems*, ed. Frederick Glaysher (New York: Liveright Publishing Corporation, 1985).

——— , *Collected Prose*, ed. Frederick Glaysher (Ann Arbor: University of Michigan Press, 1984).

Gerard Manley Hopkins, *The Poetical Works of Gerard Manley Hopkins*, ed. Norman H. MacKenzie (Oxford: Clarendon Press, 1990).

John Keats, *The Poems of John Keats*, ed. Jack Stillinger (Cambridge, MA: Belknap Press of Harvard University Press, 1978).

D. H. Lawrence, *Complete Poems*, ed. Vivian de Sola Pinto and F. Warren Roberts (New York: Penguin Books, 1993).

James Merrill, *Collected Poems*, ed. J. D. McClatchy and Stephen Yenser (New York: Alfred A. Knopf, 2001).

John Milton, *Complete Poems and Major Prose*, ed. Merritt Y. Hughes (New York: Odyssey, 1957).

Marianne Moore, *New Collected Poems*, ed. Heather Cass White (New York: Farrar, Straus and Giroux, 2017).

Sylvia Plath, *The Collected Poems*, ed. Ted Hughes (New York: Harper Perennial, 1981).

——— , *The Unabridged Journals of Sylvia Plath*, ed. Karen V. Kukil (New York: Vintage, 2000).

Adrienne Rich, *Collected Poems: 1950–2012* (New York: W. W. Norton, 2016).

Edmund Spenser, *The Faerie Queene*, ed. Thomas P. Roche Jr. and C. Patrick O'Donnell Jr. (New York: Penguin Books, 1979).

Wallace Stevens, *Collected Poetry and Prose*, ed. Frank Kermode and Joan Richardson (New York: Library of America, 1997).

Helen Vendler, *The Art of Shakespeare's Sonnets* (Cambridge, MA: Belknap Press of Harvard University Press, 1997).

Ocean Vuong, *Time Is a Mother* (New York: Penguin Press, 2022).

Walt Whitman, *Leaves of Grass and Other Writings*, ed. Michael Moon (New York: W. W. Norton, 2002).

——— , *The Walt Whitman Archive*, ed. Matt Cohen, Ed Folsom, and Kenneth M. Price, 1995–, http://www.whitmanarchive.org/.

W. B. Yeats, *The Collected Poems of W. B. Yeats*, rev. 2nd ed., ed. Richard Finneran (New York: Macmillan, 1996).

Permissions

Index

The text of this book is set in 11 point Adobe Garamond, a digital typeface designed by Robert Slimbach in 1989 for Adobe Systems and inspired by a hand-cut type created in the mid-1500s by Claude Garamond, as well as the italics produced during the same period by Robert Granjon. The display font, Silk Serif, was designed by Icelandic graphic artist Rakel Tómasdóttir and published by SilkType. Debuting in 2017, the font was updated in 2025.

The paper is acid-free and exceeds the requirements for permanence established by the American National Standards Institute.

Text design and composition by Gopa & Ted2, Inc., Albuquerque, New Mexico. Printing and binding by Lakeside Book Company.